SHARON COLLINS

BIT OF THE GOOD STUFF

Over 100 easy and delicious
plant-powered recipes
for all the family to enjoy

DEDICATED TO LUCIEN ♥

Text and Photographs: Sharon Collins
Cover and Interior Design: Catriona Archer
Illustrations: Shutterstock / Artists: Anastasia Nio, AVA Bitter, Gorbash Varvara, Natalia Hubbert, Rina_Ro, Sonya Illustration, Pim and Zabavina.
Backgrounds: Shutterstock / Artists: Digieye, Flas100, Liashko, RoyStudioEU and Schab.

ISBN: 978-1-5272-0192-7

First published in the United Kingdom in 2016
by Bit of the Good Stuff

Printed in England

Printed on Forest Stewardship Council (FSC) certified paper from forests managed in an environmentally appropriate, socially beneficial and economically viable manner.

This book is intended for information only and is not intended as a substitute for the medical advice of a doctor or physician. Before making any dietary changes, or for any matters relating to your health, it is recommended that you seek the advice of a health care professional.

Although the author has made every effort to ensure that the information in this book was correct at time of press, the author does not assume and hereby disclaims any liability to any party for any loss, damage, or disruption caused by errors or omissions, whether such errors or omissions result from negligence, accident, or any other cause.

This book is available at special discounts for bulk purchase for sales promotions, fund-raising and educational purposes. Contact: enquiries@bitofthegoodstuff.com

Contents

Introduction

I am passionate about good food! I love preparing food that not only tastes delicious and looks beautiful, but also makes us healthy, strong and happy. Fortunately, Mother Nature supplies the most incredible bounty of plants that are packed with the nutrients we need in order to thrive.

It was the birth of my son (known to my blog readers as 'Lil' L') that sparked my interest in food and nutrition. It dawned on me that I was now responsible for the well-being of another person, and this seemed such a big responsibility! Of course, like any mother, I wanted to make sure that I gave him the best start in life. I wanted to prepare food that was going to nourish him and keep him healthy. I also realised that I needed to take care of my own health so that I would be able to look after him.

Eating for Tip-Top Health

Trawling through scientific, medical and nutrition journals, I read time and again of the health benefits of a whole-food plant-based diet which focuses on eating highly nutritious foods, namely vegetables, legumes (beans, peas and lentils), whole grains, fruits, nuts and seeds. These are the foods that supply the body with the nutrients it needs for good health, including antioxidants, vitamins, minerals, fibre, complex carbohydrates and plant proteins. In particular, it appears to significantly reduce the risk of diseases that have become prevalent in the West, including heart disease, cancers, autoimmune diseases, type II diabetes and obesity.

The advice from health professionals is that a whole-food plant-based diet is not only safe for children, but it provides the best nutritional protection against disease, both in childhood and into adulthood.[1] What we eat early in life can have a powerful effect on our future health (or ill health). By educating our children on the benefits of healthy eating, and helping them identify foods that protect health and those that can harm, they will be empowered to make informed choices and establish healthy eating patterns that are likely to stay with them throughout their lives.

> *"Vegetables, grains, fruits, legumes, and nuts are the optimal foods for children. Rich in complex carbohydrates, protein, fiber, vitamins, and minerals, they form the foundation for dietary habits that support a lifetime of health." The Physicians Committee for Responsible Medicine*

Protecting the Animals and Environment

As well as the associated health benefits, eating plants helps to minimise harm to the environment and the animals that share this planet. Studies have shown that animal agriculture has a hugely damaging impact on the environment, contributing to climate change, air pollution, land and water degradation, and the reduction of biodiversity. It consumes vast quantities of natural resources, including water and fossil fuels. It is also one of the major contributors to worldwide deforestation. The United Nations 2006 report Livestock's Long Shadow concludes that the livestock sector is "one of the top two or three most significant contributors to the most serious environmental problems, at every scale from local to global".[2]

World meat production has quadrupled in the past fifty years. Each year, in the UK alone, 900 million farmed animals are slaughtered for food. Modern farming practices not only have a detrimental impact on the environment, but these intensive ways of raising, farming and slaughtering livestock contribute significantly to the suffering of animals. A growing number of 'zero grazing units' are appearing in the UK, where animals are kept in warehouse-size sheds and never see the light of day. Each year, thousands upon thousands of male calves and chicks are slaughtered as by-products of the dairy and egg industries.

Eating with Variety and Abundance

Healthy eating doesn't have to be restrictive or a chore. In fact, our experience has been the opposite! Since going whole-food plant-based, my family is eating a greater variety of foods than ever before, and our dishes are always filled with a riot of colours, textures and flavours. In the past, we used to eat the same meals on a two-weekly rotation; these days it's rare for us to eat the same meal twice in one month. We've discovered so many fruits, vegetables, whole grains, legumes, beans, nuts, seeds, spices and herbs available in our shops - each with their own special health-protecting properties - and we're having so much fun experimenting with them and trying out new recipes.

A whole-food plant-based diet also means we can eat abundantly and not worry about counting calories. This is a big plus point for food lovers like me! Plants are less calorific and lower in saturated fats than meat, dairy and eggs, which means we can eat larger portion sizes and desserts with every meal. And rather than gaining pounds, we gain bonus nutrients and better health!

Dispelling the Protein and Calcium Myths

People often ask where we get our protein and calcium from when eating a plant-based diet so, before I go any further, I should address these two important questions. Many of us were taught in school that a diet without meat is lacking in protein, but this just isn't true. Plant foods contain plenty of protein, and providing that we eat a varied diet we are certain to get enough. Plant proteins are healthier than meat, dairy and egg proteins as they come packaged with fibre and other disease-fighting nutrients. They are low in saturated fat and cholesterol-free. Gorillas, hippos, rhinos, elephants and giraffes thrive on plant proteins, and so do humans!

We've also been led to believe that we need to consume dairy in order to obtain calcium to keep our bones strong. Again, this just isn't true. Studies show strong links between rates of hip fracture and osteoporosis and the consumption of dairy, but the opposite to what you may expect. It is the countries with the *lowest levels* of dairy consumption that have the *lowest rates* of hip fracture and osteoporosis, and the countries with the *highest levels* of dairy consumption that have the *highest rates*. The World Health Organisation refers to this as the 'Calcium Paradox'.[3] Dairy clearly isn't protecting bone health. One possible explanation is that animal protein increases the acid load in the body and, in order to neutralise this acid, the body uses its calcium stores.[4]

Many vegetables, fruits, nuts, seeds and legumes contain usable calcium. Amongst the richest sources are leafy greens, tofu, fortified plant-based milks and yogurts, edamame beans, white beans, almonds, sesame seeds, tahini and oranges.

The Benefits we've experienced so far

My son is almost thirteen years old now and continues to have bundles of energy, sleep well and have a happy disposition. To date, he has never needed antibiotics, never experienced a sore throat and he made it through six years of primary school without a single day off through ill health. He has just completed his first year at senior school, again without a single illness or day off. He enjoys eating a wide variety of plant-based foods and always approaches meal times with great enthusiasm. He already seems to be 'in tune' with his body, and very aware of how different types of foods make him feel.

Personally, I've been amazed at the extent to which my own health and well-being has improved since I made the transition to a whole-food plant-based diet. My energy levels have noticeably increased and illness has been a rarity. Prior to going plant-based, I had regular bouts of sinusitis that required antibiotics. Since making the transition, I've had no sinusitis nor needed any medication. Within days of quitting dairy, my skin became clear, I stopped having breakouts of eczema and the stomach cramps, bloating and aching joints that I'd endured for years completely disappeared. I felt like a new woman! Within six months of going whole-food plant-based, I lost 10 pounds (4.5 kilos). Since then, my weight has remained constant but my body shape has changed. I'm still doing the same amount of exercise, but I'm noticeably leaner.

My husband has also had positive experiences since transitioning to a whole-food plant-based diet. A keen mountain biker for over twenty years, he's now got more stamina and riding faster than ever before. Now in our mid-forties, both my husband and I feel healthier, fitter and stronger than ever. Neither of us imagined that we would feel this good at the age we are now. Far from 'over the hill', we feel that we're still on our way up!

Bit of the Good Stuff

I started writing my blog 'Bit of the Good Stuff' back in 2010. It was a place to collect and share plant-based recipes that we'd tried and loved, and especially those that were a 'hit' with Lil' L. Yet blogging has given me much more than this. It has brought me into contact with so many supportive, caring individuals from all over the world. I am bearing witness to the growing popularity of compassionate lifestyles. It's a movement that's rapidly gathering momentum and I'm thrilled to be part of it.

While I regularly post recipes online, I've received numerous requests for a compilation of recipes in book form. Despite the explosion of online recipe sites, it's clear that people still love recipe books. I can totally appreciate where they're coming from. So, for the past five years, I've been compiling and photographing a selection of my family's all-time favourite plant-based recipes. With the exception of a couple of special desserts, the recipes featured in this book are very much 'every day' recipes. They are simple to make and budget-friendly. These are the kinds of recipes that my family eats 'day in day out'. They are fully tried and tested, not only by my family, but also by over fifty international recipe testers.

You may be interested in eating plant-based meals once or twice a week, perhaps joining in worldwide initiatives such as 'Meat-free Monday'. On the other hand, you may like the idea of eating plant-based meals for the majority of the time or cutting out animal products altogether. The choice is entirely yours. Any increase in whole-food plant-based meals is going to have a positive impact on your health and the environment. If you're interested in finding out more about the benefits of plant-based eating, I've compiled a recommended list of reading, online and film resources at the end of the book.

I wish you lots of fun and fulfilment exploring the world of whole-food plant-based cooking. It's been such a rewarding experience for me, as I hope it will be for you too!

Encouraging Kids to Love their Veggies

I know how challenging it can be to get kids to eat their veggies. In fact, pretty much every kid I've known has gone through a 'picky phase'. The important thing is not to stress over it. They will grow out of it. Some just take longer than others. If you want to give them a helpful nudge in the right direction, you'll find lots of tips on the internet. Here are a few that worked for me.

1   **Start young.** As soon as they reach the weaning stage, introduce them to a wide selection of raw and cooked vegetables so that their taste buds get used to a variety of tastes and textures.

2   **Prepare one meal for all the family.** Serving children different meals to the adults could give them the impression that children eat different foods, thus making them less inclined to try 'adult' dishes. This potential pitfall can be avoided by preparing the same meal for the whole family. Since children have more sensitive taste buds than adults, keep the seasonings light then, once the children's portions have been served, add more spice for the adults. For young children, chop the veggies finely or blitz them with a hand blender. As they get older, gradually increase the size of the pieces.

3   **Eat as a family.** Whenever possible, eat evening and weekend meals together. Lil' L was always far more likely to try a new dish or vegetable if he saw us enthusiastically tucking into it.

4   **Keep an open mind.** When Lil' L said he didn't like a particular vegetable, I didn't make a fuss or try and make him eat it. I just told him that as he got older, his taste buds would develop and he would start to like more foods. Maybe he could try that vegetable again when he was a little older? By giving this explanation, I was trying to keep his mind open so that he wouldn't think 'I don't like this vegetable and I never will'. It seemed to do the trick. By the age of seven, he was eating a multitude of vegetables that in previous years, he'd not liked.

5   **Get sneaky.** I used to blitz unpopular veggies with the hand blender so they were hidden in the dinner (I'm sure a lot of parents have used this trick). Each time I made the dinner, I would gradually chop the vegetables less and less fine. We've had such a huge turn around with onions and mushrooms. He used to sift through his dinner and pick out every little piece. Now they're amongst his favourite vegetables!

6   **Dress up salads.** Leaves (especially romaine lettuce, radicchio, rocket and spinach) and other colourful salad ingredients are packed with phytonutrients, antioxidants, vitamins, minerals and fibre, so it's good to get into the habit of eating at least one portion of salad a day. To encourage kids to eat their leaves, serve them with a generous dollop of hummus or a healthy salad dressing. Slice raw veggies such as cucumber, pepper and carrot into sticks and serve them as snacks or a starter, along with a bowl of their favourite dip.

7   **Explain the health benefits.** When Lil' L was small, I found that he was far more likely to tuck into a vegetable if I'd explained the specific nutrients it contains and how they help his body. This approach proved far more effective than the 'eat it up, it's good for you' response. I guess it's like anything in life - if we know the specific benefits of something, we're definitely more inclined to give it a try.

8   Experiment with different food preparations. Raw, steamed, roasted, whole, blended - there are so many ways to prepare foods and when a child says that they dislike a particular vegetable, it could simply be a particular serving style they dislike rather than the vegetable itself. This is something I learned early on with Lil' L. For example, he disliked cooked carrot, but he loved raw carrot sticks (especially when served with hummus). Raw or steamed kale definitely got a thumbs down, but he loved 'crispy kale' and kale soup. As long as they're eating nutritious foods, it doesn't really matter how they go down!

9   Get the kids involved. Children are far more enthusiastic about eating vegetables when they've helped to pick and prepare them. If you have the space, you could grow your own veggies. Herbs in pots on the windowsill is an easy place to start. Visit farmer's markets or the local grocers and invite the children to choose a new vegetable to try each week. Back home, they can help you prepare a meal with it.

10   Have themed meals. To encourage kids to try new vegetables and dishes, organise 'theme nights'. It could be 'Foods from around the World' where they take it in turns to pick a country, then help prepare a traditional dish from that country, or it could be a weekly 'Alphabet Challenge' where the children take it in turns to pick a new vegetable and cook a meal with it, working their way through the alphabet.

11   Give vegetables fun names. 'X Ray Vision Carrots', 'Power Punch Broccoli', 'Silly Dilly Green Beans' - a study of US elementary school cafeterias found that the purchase of vegetables increased by almost *100%* when they were given fun, kid-appealing names.[5] How incredible is that?

12   And finally, if all else fails, blend! Soups are a great way to encourage kids to eat a big pile of veggies. You can even sneak spinach into a smoothie and they won't detect it. Check out Lil' L's favourite 'Friendly Green Monster' smoothie on p35.

A Few of my Favourite Ingredients

I'm sure that most of the ingredients in my recipes will be familiar to you. They are widely available and easy to pick up in grocery stores. However, there is a small bunch of ingredients which are less 'mainstream' right now and may be new to you. I love these ingredients for their unique taste, texture, nutritional content or all of the above! These ingredients are definitely worth seeking out! In the UK, they can be purchased in health food stores and online. They are also slowly making their way into our supermarkets.

Buckwheat (aka Buckwheat Groats)

Despite its misleading name, buckwheat doesn't contain any wheat or gluten. Nor is it a grain. It is a fruit seed! It has a great nutritional profile. It is a good source of protein (containing all the essential amino acids), dietary fibre, antioxidant phytonutrients, B vitamins and minerals. We love to add raw buckwheat to our granolas (p26-p29) as it gives them crunch as well as an extra dose of nutrients. In the UK, buckwheat is currently available in some supermarkets (Tesco, Waitrose, Ocado), health food stores and online.

Cacao Powder and Nibs

Cacao powder is made from raw cacao beans, while cocoa powder is made from roasted beans. Of the two, cacao powder is the most nutrient dense. It is packed with antioxidants and minerals, including iron, magnesium, zinc and manganese. It also contains mood-enhancing serotonin, phenylethamine (PEA) (the 'love' chemical) and anandamide (the 'bliss' chemical). Cacao nibs are cacao beans that have been broken into smaller pieces. They are bitter, chocolatey and nutty. In the UK, cacao powder and nibs are currently available in health food stores and online.

Chia Seeds

The chia seed comes from the Salvia Hispanica, a beautiful flowering plant from the mint family. It is rich in protein, dietary fibre, B vitamins, minerals (including iron, calcium and zinc) and omega 3 essential fatty acids. It's easily digested and absorbs more than nine times its weight in liquid when soaked, helping to regulate blood sugar levels and hydration. I find it has an amazing satiating quality and just one tablespoon blended into a smoothie will leave me feeling full up for hours. Since I started writing this book, the availability of chia seeds has become much wider in the UK, and they can now be found in the major supermarkets as well as health food stores and online.

Culinary/Aroma-Free Coconut Butter

For pastry-making, I like to use organic culinary/aroma-free coconut butter. It's less processed than vegetable spread/vegan butter, and makes pastry nice and crisp without leaving your fingers greasy (like oil-based pastries). Coconut butter includes the coconut meat as well as the oil, so it's thicker and creamier than coconut oil. In the UK, culinary/aroma-free coconut butter is currently available from health food stores and online.

Coconut Sugar (aka Coconut Palm Sugar, Coconut Blossom)

I do try to minimise the sugar content in my recipes but, if a dry sweetener is called for, my number one choice is coconut sugar. This sugar is produced from the flower buds of the coconut palm tree and has a delicious caramel-like flavour. While cane sugar can give me a churning tummy sensation and leave me feeling nauseous, I feel no ill effects from coconut sugar. In the UK, it is currently available from Ocado, in health food stores and online.

Creamed Coconut

Creamed coconut is pure coconut flesh that has been pulverised and formed into solid blocks. I love using it in Asian curries and soups to add creaminess and a touch of sweetness. In the UK, it can be found in large supermarkets (in the world food aisle), health food stores and Asian supermarkets. If you're unable to find creamed coconut where you live, coconut butter can be used as an alternative.

Hemp Seeds, Shelled (aka Hemp Hearts)

Though hemp seeds come from a variety of cannabis sativa, the plant contains extremely low levels (0.02% or less) of tetrahydrocannabinol (THC). Here in the UK, it's legal to grow hemp for culinary purposes. The seeds are a rich source of protein, minerals (especially magnesium, zinc and iron) and omega 3 essential fatty acids. They are also a natural source of Gamma Linolenic Acid (GLA), which has powerful anti-inflammatory properties. In the UK, hemp seeds are currently available from Ocado, health food stores and online.

Lemongrass

Lemongrass is a fragrant tropical grass widely used in Asian cooking. In UK supermarkets, it is usually found in the fresh herb section. The fragrance and flavour is unique - lemony but sweet - and quite subtle until the stalk is cut or bruised. You can use lemongrass whole, sliced or blended into a paste. To use whole stalks, cut off the woody end, remove any tough outer leaves, then 'bruise' by bashing with a rolling pin or bending to soften and release the aromatic oils. Lemongrass can be stored in the refrigerator for a few days or for weeks in the freezer.

Millet

I used to think millet was reserved for birds, but it's actually a delicious grain and perfectly fit for human consumption! It has a mild nutty, corn flavour and a fluffy, slightly sticky texture that is not dissimilar to couscous. Since millet is gluten-free, I find it makes a great gluten-free substitute for couscous in Moroccan and Caribbean dishes. It contains a wide range of B vitamins and minerals, as well as protein and dietary fibre. In the UK, millet is currently available from health food stores and online.

Miso

A staple of Japanese cuisine, miso is a fermented paste made of soya beans, barley, rice or chickpeas. Brown miso adds a deep, savoury 'umami' flavour to soups and stews. It is rich in minerals, antioxidant phytonutrients and 'friendly' bacteria. White Miso (aka Sweet Miso, Shiro Miso) is made with cultured rice and whole soya beans. It is fermented for a shorter time and lower in sodium than darker varieties. It has a creamy texture and delicate salty-sweet flavour, which makes it perfect for creamy pasta sauces (p104) and gravies (p141). White miso is less common in the UK than brown miso. I use Clearspring Organic Japanese Sweet White Miso which is currently available from Waitrose, Ocado, health food stores and online.

Nori Flakes

Sea vegetables are one of the richest sources of minerals available. We often use a sprinkling of nori flakes to season savoury dishes such as paella (p114). They're a great way to boost our intake of trace minerals iodine and selenium, which are more difficult to source from land vegetables. We use Clearspring Japanese Green Nori Sprinkle, currently available in the UK from health food stores and online.

Nutritional Yeast Flakes

Nutritional yeast is an inactive yeast which has a delicious savoury flavour, often described as both 'nutty' and 'cheesy'. We use it to enhance the savouriness of casseroles, soups and frittatas, as well as a dairy-free alternative to parmesan (p101). It has a fantastic nutritional profile and is packed with B vitamins, folic acid and zinc. It is also a good source of protein, with a 10g serving providing 10% of the recommended daily amount (RDA). We use the Marigold Engevita Savoury Yeast Condiment fortified with vitamin B12. Just a 5g serving provides 220% of the B12 RDA. In the UK, it is currently available from health food stores and online.

Tahini (Sesame Paste)

Tahini - a paste made from ground sesame seeds - is an essential component of hummus. It also happens to be packed with nutritional goodness. It contains a whole host of minerals (including calcium and iron), as well as cholesterol-lowering phytosterols. I find that shop-bought tahini can vary considerably in flavour and consistency. My favourite brand is Achva (available in the UK from Tesco and Morrisons). This tahini has a great flavour and creamy consistency, making it perfect for dips and dressings.

Eating Organic

Prior to the 1940s, organic farming methods were the norm. Unfortunately, the move towards intensive farming practices was accompanied by the arrival of chemical agriculture, which has resulted in serious damage to the environment, including water pollution, soil degradation, and a reduction in biodiversity.

Not only is organic food better for the environment, but it is better for our health too. Most commercial crops are sprayed with an array of herbicides, pesticides, fungicides and rodent killers, and the residues of these chemicals can be found in produce. Whenever possible, I will buy organic produce, especially berries, apples, celery, bell peppers, tomatoes, leafy greens and cucumber as these retain some of the highest levels of pesticide residue. I also prioritise vegetables that I tend not to peel, like potatoes and carrots.

It is possible to eat organic on a budget, especially when eating plant-based meals as they tend to be far cheaper than meat and fish-based dishes. It's even cheaper if you're lucky enough to grow your own, have a local community produce sharing scheme, or have friends with their own allotment space. I find that green-fingered friends often have a surplus of fruits and vegetables in late summer and are more than happy to share. They're even more delighted when I offer to share home-made goodies in return!

While I've struggled to grow veggies myself due to the thousands of critters that live in my garden, I have found it easy to grow my own herbs. Rosemary, sage, mint and flat leaf parsley grow well in my garden. Snails are partial to basil though, so I keep it on the kitchen window ledge where they can't reach it!

We've also had some success growing fruits. We have one small plum tree, a tiny eating apple tree (which grows in a rockery!) and a larger cooking apple tree. We also have blackberry bushes growing wild in the garden. For me, nothing beats eating produce from your own garden. It doesn't get more organic or fresh than that!

My Kitchen Equipment Essentials

I remember the days when the only kitchen gadgets I owned were a kettle, toaster and sandwich maker! In recent years, a few more gadgets have crept into my kitchen. Most of them have been really useful and get used multiple times a week. Here are a few that I would definitely recommend:

Powerful High Speed Blender
In our house, the jug blender gets used daily for making smoothies, soups, sauces and puddings. If you can afford the initial outlay, it's definitely worth investing in a power blender. It will pulverise veggies, fruits, nuts and seeds in a matter of seconds, plus it will easily outlast cheaper blenders, saving money in the long run. I've been using a Froothie blender (Optimum 9400) for a couple of years now and I've been really impressed with its quality and power. If you want to find out more, there is a full review of the blender on my blog, plus details of how to receive a free seven-year warranty via my reader offer.

Hand Blender (aka Immersion or Stick Blender)
I bought a hand blender for puréeing baby food, but a decade later it's still an essential piece of equipment in my kitchen. I use it multiple times a week for making small batches of hummus and pesto, curry pastes, fresh fruit yogurts, waffles and pancakes. The bowl attachment that came with my blender is perfect for blending small quantities that would fly around inside a larger food processor.

Food Processor
I didn't actually own a food processor until I turned 40, but now I couldn't imagine life without one. It gets used multiple times a week for making hummus, pesto, nut roasts, bread crumbs, energy bites, 'cheesecakes' and banana ice cream. Four years ago, I treated myself to a Magimix. It is a sturdy piece of kit and the motor has a twelve year guarantee, which should make it a good investment.

Electric Coffee/Spice Grinder
I use an electric grinder for grinding linseed (flaxseed), spices (like cumin and coriander) and for making Cashew 'Parmesan' (p101) and Gomasio (p185). It's far quicker than a mortar and pestle and grinds the nuts, seeds and spices super fine.

Kitchen Scales
When baking, I always use kitchen scales so that the ingredients are measured accurately. I use Salter Aquatronic digital scales which enable you to weigh all your dry and liquid ingredients in one bowl. They're not very expensive and I can highly recommend them.

Measuring Cups

When it comes to breakfasts and smoothie making, I find it much quicker to measure the ingredients in cups rather than weighing them. I own multiple sets of cups, but my favourites are stainless steel. Unlike plastic cups, they don't flip over in the dishwasher!

Measuring Spoons

I used to estimate a teaspoon, half teaspoon, tablespoon and so forth, and sometimes my estimates would be way off. This resulted in cakes that would rise super high then collapse in the middle and pancakes with more holes than Swiss cheese! A couple of years ago, my mum bought me a set of measuring spoons and I've used them every day since.

Fine Grater

I use a lot of ginger and citrus zest, and a quality fine grater makes this food preparation a breeze. Microplanes are very effective, but can be extremely sharp so watch your fingers! I currently use the Oxo Good Grips Grater which is less sharp than a microplane but does the job. Most importantly for me, it grates ginger without leaving a handful of stringy fibres (unlike my old box grater).

Garlic Press

I use garlic almost every day and the easiest way I've found to 'mince' it is to use a garlic press. It literally takes a couple of seconds.

Quality Knives

I find that a decent knife can make all the difference to the experience of food preparation. For over fifteen years now, I've been using the same utility knife (John Lewis brand). It has a 12.5cm blade and serrated edge. It cuts through veggies effortlessly, even butternut squash skin. It's definitely worth investing in a decent knife. It'll save you a lot of hassle and time, as well as your skin. A quality, sharp knife is much safer than hacking away at vegetables with a cheap, blunt one.

For chopping nuts and herbs, nothing beats a knife with a curved blade. Rock the blade back and forth over them, and they chop fine in a matter of seconds. I bought my curved blade knife fourteen years ago from a cookery school in Thailand (it cost me the grand sum of 50 pence). You'll find similar (slightly more expensive) models in kitchen and homeware stores.

Bread Maker

Okay, so this isn't an essential piece of kitchen equipment, but I find my bread maker really handy, especially for making pizza dough (p136) and Monkey Bread (p48). You simply throw the ingredients in the bowl, press the button and 45 minutes later, the dough is ready. The cost of our machine has easily been covered by the savings we've made on choosing to make home-made pizzas rather than eating out. We often set up the machine on a Friday evening before we head out for a drink. When we return home, the dough is ready and waiting for us.

Getting Started

Prepping Ingredients - 'Mise-en-place'

When trying a recipe for the first time, it's best to prepare all the ingredients before you start cooking. Chefs call this 'mise-en-place'. It makes the cooking experience far more relaxed and enjoyable. Once you're familiar with a recipe, you may prefer to prep the ingredients as you go along. Keep a bowl alongside your ingredients for collecting the peelings and scraps. This will help keep your worktop tidy and save multiple trips to your compost bin.

'Hands on' and 'Ready in' Times

Before I begin a recipe, I like to know how long it will take to complete and how much time I'll personally be involved. This helps me determine which recipes are suitable for busy weekdays or how long in advance I need to start preparing dinner in order to serve it at a specific time. In my recipes, **'Hands on'** indicates the amount of time that you will be involved in the prepping and cooking of the meal, while **'Ready in'** indicates the total amount of time the recipe takes, from preparation through to completion.

Weighing and Measuring Ingredients

TBSP = tablespoon   Tsp = teaspoon

Unless otherwise stated, all TBSP and tsp measurements refer to **level** tablespoons and teaspoons. Similarly, all cup measurements refer to **level** cups unless otherwise stated.

Kitchen Scales vs Measuring Cups

Depending on the type of recipe that I'm making, I use either kitchen scales or measuring cups. All my recipes work with either metric or imperial cups. The important thing is to stick with one set of measuring devices when following a recipe so that you keep the proportions correct.

While measuring cups are fine for recipes where the ingredient quantities don't have to be too precise, when it comes to baking, I highly recommend using kitchen scales. I find that quantities of foods (flour, in particular) can vary immensely when you measure them in a cup and, for baking, it's important to achieve the correct ratio of dry and wet ingredients. Flour can become quite densely packed in its bag, so if you're planning on using cups, be sure to loosen up the flour before you scoop it. For me, on average, one cup of flour weighs 140g.

Choosing Plant-Based Milks

Many people choose to avoid dairy, whether it be due to health, environmental or ethical reasons. Fortunately, plant-based alternatives to cow's milk are now widely available and there are plenty to choose from including soya, almond, hazelnut, cashew, rice, oat, hemp and coconut drinking milks. All have their own unique taste (and also vary depending on brand), so it's worth trying them out and seeing which ones suit your taste buds.

Soya milk is my favourite milk for baking. It curdles when whisked with vinegar to produce a dairy-free alternative to butter milk, resulting in light and fluffy bakes. Soya milk also works exceptionally well in pancakes (p38-p40), with no need for the usual resting time for the batter. I also find soya milk is the best plant-based milk for tea and coffee, while rice milk makes a delicious drink on its own. My family usually has a couple of different milks in the refrigerator at any one time. To boost our calcium, vitamin D and B12 intake, we choose to buy fortified milks.

Since the milks vary in flavour and consistency, in my recipes I will specify if a certain milk is required, otherwise I will use the term 'non-dairy milks' to denote that any plant-based milk can be used.

Nuts and Seeds

Nuts and seeds are good sources of protein, heart-healthy fats and minerals. Walnuts, ground linseed (flaxseed), chia seeds and hemp seeds are rich in omega-3 and we tend to consume these on a daily basis. While we eat most nuts and seeds in their raw form, we do keep toasted flaked almonds and sesame seeds in the pantry to garnish savoury dishes. Toasted flaked almonds are widely available in UK supermarkets but sesame seeds we toast at home. The easiest way to do this is to dry fry them in a frying pan (skillet) on medium heat for a couple of minutes, stirring continuously. As soon as they start to brown, tip onto a plate. Leave to cool then transfer to an airtight jar where they will keep for months.

If your house is cool, nuts and seeds can be stored in airtight jars in the pantry. However, if your house is on the warm side, it is best to store them in the refrigerator to stop them going rancid.

Soya Beans, Edamame and Tofu

Like their fellow legumes, soya beans are actually seeds of a plant. They have been cultivated in China for well over 13,000 years, and are a staple in traditional Asian diets from childhood. Soya is rich in protein (it contains all the essential amino acids), antioxidant phytonutrients, B vitamins and minerals. It also contains phytosterols which can help lower cholesterol levels.

Two ways that my family enjoys consuming soya is in the form of edamame and tofu. Edamame (green soya beans) make a tasty, nutritiously-rich snack. Pots of fresh, ready-to-eat edamame and frozen bags are available in supermarkets and health food stores. To prepare frozen edamame, boil in a pan of water for a couple of minutes, drain, then add a light sprinkling of salt and serve.

Tofu (soya bean curd) is a versatile ingredient that can be used in both sweet and savoury dishes. Firm tofu is typically found in the chiller cabinets of grocery stores and comes packed in water. Once drained, it can be crumbled to make scrambled tofu (p69), blended to make tofu 'ricotta' (p139), pressed and pan-fried in oil or pressed, marinated and baked (p20). You can also buy a variety of pre-marinated and smoked tofus. As well as making a tasty addition to Asian dishes, they're also great as sandwich fillings.

Silken tofu is much softer and creamier than firm tofu. It's usually found in tetra paks in the world food aisles of grocery stores. I love using silken tofu as an egg-replacer in frittatas (p72).

How to Press and Cook Tofu

There are various techniques for pressing firm tofu. Some people use tea cloths or paper towels to absorb the water, while others invest in tofu presses. If you don't have a tofu press, here is a method that minimises mess, waste and cost:

Split the pack open along one edge, drain off the water, then slice the block through the middle into two equal halves. Arrange the tofu on a large rimmed baking sheet or lipped tea tray. Place a chopping board on top of the tofu, followed by a heavy object to weigh it down. The longer you press the tofu, the firmer it will become; 30 minutes to an hour is preferable. The water will have collected in a pool round the tofu, so drain it off, pat the tofu with some kitchen paper to mop up any residual liquid, and you're good to go.

If you're planning to add the tofu to a sauce (like Sweet 'n' Sour p109), you can simply pan fry it in a little oil with a light sprinkling of salt until golden brown. This will give the tofu a lovely, crispy exterior with a softer centre. For other dishes, you may want to marinate the tofu to steep it in flavour, then bake it. Baking tofu gives it a firmer texture compared to pan frying.

Marinated Baked Tofu

Marinated tofu is great for topping Asian soups, such as our Japanese Miso Noodle Soup (p64) and Malaysian Coconut Noodle Soup (p61), and for stuffing into pittas and wraps. The recipe below is my 'go to' tofu marinade which uses ingredients that I always have on hand. Once marinated, the tofu is baked in the oven to give it a firm, chewy texture.

Serves: 3-4   Hands on: 10 minutes   Ready in: 1 hour 35 minutes

1 block of firm tofu (about 400g / 14 oz)
3 TBSP tamari or reduced-salt soy sauce
2 TBSP apple cider vinegar
1 tsp tomato purée (paste)

1-2 tsp sweet chilli sauce (omit for children)
2 TBSP water
2 garlic cloves, minced

1   Press the tofu for 30 minutes (p19).

2   Mix all the marinade ingredients together in a wide, shallow container.

3   Cube the tofu and add it to the marinade. Tilt the dish, left, right, back and forth, so that the marinade coats all sides of the tofu cubes. Leave the tofu to soak for 30 minutes. Tilt the dish now and then to re-coat the cubes.

4   Preheat the oven to 200C (180C fan) / 400F. Line a large baking sheet with non-stick baking paper.

5   Arrange the tofu on the prepared sheet and place in the oven for 30 minutes, or until lightly browned. Flip the cubes over halfway through the cooking time.

6   Store the tofu in an airtight container in the refrigerator for up to five days.

Freezing Food

Freezing food can be a fantastic time and money saver. I have four drawers in my freezer, which I divide up as follows:

Drawer 1 - Frozen Fruits

I always have a large stash of bananas, mango chunks and berries in the freezer. These are used for making smoothies, sorbets, ice creams and fruity yogurts. I buy an extra bunch of bananas each week specifically for freezing. I leave them in the fruit bowl until they are spotted brown, then peel them, and transfer them to freezer bags. They're easy to slice when frozen, so I freeze them whole to save time and space.

Mango chunks, blueberries and raspberries are bought pre-frozen. Whenever possible, I buy organic berries (available, in the UK, from health food stores). Organic strawberries are bought fresh, then sliced and arranged in a single layer in a freezer bag (this prevents them from freezing together in a big clump).

I also store citrus zest in this freezer drawer. Organic/unwaxed citrus fruits can be expensive so, if I only need to use the flesh in a recipe, I first zest the fruit, press it into a half tablespoon or teaspoon so that it sticks together, then transfer it to a small container in the freezer. This way, there is no waste and I have zest on hand for recipes like Florentines (p172), Spiced Orange Oatmeal Raisin Cookies (p168) and Bread Pudding (p158).

Drawer 2 - Frozen Vegetables

I use this drawer for storing vegetables that are easy to bulk purchase in freezer bags, out of season vegetables and convenience foods. On a typical day, you'll find green peas, fine green beans, cauliflower florets, edamame beans in pods, bags of mixed vegetables and meat-free mince in there.

I also use this drawer for storing home-made pestos, curry pastes and curry paste ingredients – red chillies, lemongrass, coriander leaves (cilantro) and root ginger (chopped into 1 inch chunks). I find that root ginger grates easily from frozen, so there is no need to defrost it. Frozen chillies also slice easily.

Drawer 3 - Baked Goods, Treats & Sweets

This drawer contains shop-bought bread items (pitta breads, tortilla wraps, rolls), as well as home-made goods such as cookies, cakes and chocolates. Frosted cakes can be frozen. Simply leave them in the refrigerator until the frosting is firm to the touch, then place them in freezer bags, gently squeeze out the air (to prevent freezer burn) and secure. I try to use home-baked goods within four weeks of freezing to prevent any deterioration in the flavours. 'Cheesecakes' and chocolates will keep for a couple of months.

Drawer 4 - Pre-cooked Savoury Dishes

Most of my savoury recipes are suitable for freezing, so I often freeze any leftovers in airtight glass or plastic containers. These are great to pull out on days when there is little time to prepare and cook a meal from scratch. I try to use pre-cooked savoury dishes within six weeks of freezing to prevent any deterioration in the flavours.

Breakfast & Elevenses

Breakfast is often deemed the most important meal of the day and, from personal experience, I have to agree. Starting the day with a high quality breakfast, I feel fired up and ready to take on the world. I never get hunger pangs nor need a mid morning snack. On the other hand, if I skip breakfast or eat something too light, my energy levels are noticeably lower, I can't think so clearly and my tummy soon starts rumbling.

It's really important that we power ourselves up in the morning with a healthy breakfast, and encourage our kids to do the same. Instead of sugary cereals which can induce energy spikes and slumps (and affect concentration), opt for whole grains like oats. Mixed with your favourite nuts, seeds and fruits, these nutrient-rich breakfasts will boost your mood, provide lots of slow release energy and keep you sustained all morning.

In this chapter, you'll find a selection of my family's favourite breakfasts. On weekday mornings, we love tucking into porridge, overnight oats, granola, muesli, ice cream breakfast bowls and 'breakfast in a glass' smoothies, while pancakes, waffles and baked goodies make tasty weekend treats.

Pick 'n' Mix Breakfast Toppers

I love those breakfast buffet bars in hotels where you can choose an array of fruits, nuts and seeds to add to your muesli bowl. I imagine you're meant to choose one or two toppings, but I walk along the buffet line sprinkling a little bit of everything into my bowl. The end result is a big bowl of beautiful colours, shapes and textures.

One day I got to thinking how easy it would be to re-create the Pick 'n' Mix bar at home. I washed out some old glass jars and filled them with our favourite nuts, seeds and dried fruits. It's been a real success and the Pick 'n' Mix jars get used every day, not just for muesli, but for topping our overnight oats, porridge, pancakes, chia puddings and ice cream bowls. The great thing about the Pick 'n' Mix jars is that each family member can tailor their breakfast to suit their own individual tastes.

Fill glass jars with your favourite nuts, seeds and dried fruits to create your own Pick 'n' Mix bar. All of the following make great additions to breakfast bowls:

★ nuts (e.g. walnuts, pecans, toasted flaked almonds, chopped brazil nuts)

★ seeds (e.g. pumpkin seeds, toasted sunflower seeds, ground linseed (flaxseed), chia seeds)

★ dried fruits (e.g. goji berries, cranberries, chopped dates, chopped apricots, raisins)

TIP The Pick 'n' Mix jars are also handy for creating your own trail mixes. Stash a pot in your bag for an easy, portable snack.

Chocolate Porridge

Serves: 1   Hands on: 5 minutes   Ready in: 7 minutes

When it comes to making porridge, rather than weighing the ingredients, we find it's far quicker to use a cup. As a rule of thumb, we use a ratio of ½ cup oats: 1 cup of milk per person. However, everyone has their own preference when it comes to porridge consistency, so do adjust the ratio to suit your own tastes. We love to top our porridge with nuts, seeds and dried fruits from our Pick 'n' Mix jars (see opposite).

50g / ½ cup rolled oats
1 TBSP cocoa powder
240ml / 1 cup non-dairy milk

½ TBSP maple syrup, or to taste
1 tsp ground linseed (flaxseed), optional for a nutrient boost
Pick 'n' Mix toppings (p24)

1   Add the oats and cocoa powder to a pan and stir through to combine. Stir in the milk. Bring to the boil, then reduce the heat and simmer for 3 minutes, or until the oats are tender. Stir continuously to prevent the porridge sticking to the pan. Add maple syrup, to taste.

2   Transfer to a bowl, then leave to cool for a couple of minutes (the porridge will thicken as it cools). Stir in 1 tsp ground linseed, if desired. Sprinkle on your toppings of choice and serve.

TIP   The consistency of your porridge will vary depending on the type of plant-based milk used, so do experiment to discover which ones you prefer. Amongst our favourites are soya, rice and almond milk.

THE GOOD STUFF ♥
Pecans are a great source of dietary fibre and heart-healthy monounsaturated fats. They are rich in antioxidant phytonutrients and a wide range of minerals, including manganese, magnesium and zinc.

Maple Pecan Granola Clusters

Makes: 10 servings   Hands on: 10 minutes   Ready in: 60 minutes

Most commercial granolas are laden with refined sugars and oils, so why not ditch them and prepare your own delicious, healthier version instead? Granola is so simple to make and takes only a few minutes to prepare. In fact, it's so easy that the kids can make their own.

300g / 3 cups rolled oats

100g / ½ cup buckwheat (p10)

40g / 4 TBSP fine wholemeal (whole wheat pastry) flour, chapatti flour or gluten-free (GF) flour mix

30g / ⅓ cup desiccated coconut

60g / ½ cup pecans, roughly chopped

30g / ¼ cup flaked almonds

30g / 3 TBSP coconut sugar or unrefined cane sugar

½-1 tsp ground cinnamon

pinch of ground nutmeg

¼ tsp salt

150ml / ½ cup maple syrup

45g / 3 TBSP virgin coconut oil, melted

1   Preheat the oven to 150C (130C fan) / 300F. Line a large baking tray (38 x 26cm / 15 x 10 inches) with non-stick baking paper. If your coconut oil is solid, place it in a heat-proof bowl in the oven for a couple of minutes to melt it (be careful when you remove it as the container will be very hot!)

2   In a large bowl, mix together the oats, buckwheat, flour, desiccated coconut, nuts, sugar, cinnamon, nutmeg and salt. Stir in the maple syrup. Pour in the coconut oil and stir until the grains are thoroughly coated.

3   Spread the granola out evenly on the prepared baking tray and press down hard so that the mixture sticks together as if you were making a very thin granola bar. Bake for 40 minutes, until the granola has lightly browned. Remove from the oven and allow to completely cool (the granola will firm up as it cools).

4   Break up the granola into clusters. (Don't worry if the pieces from the centre of the tray still feel a little soft as I find they firm up over time). Transfer to an airtight container and store in a cool place.

5   This granola is delicious served with non-dairy milk or yogurt, and a sprinkling of your favourite dried fruits, nuts and seeds. I often add a sprinkling of chopped walnuts, ground linseed and goji berries.

TIP Layered with fresh berries and yogurt, this granola also makes a delicious parfait that can be served for breakfast or dessert.

Chocolate Hazelnut Granola Clusters

Makes: 10 servings   Hands on: 10 minutes   Ready in: 60 minutes

Filled with hazelnuts, pecans, cranberries and chocolatey goodness, this has to be the perfect granola for autumn/winter. It's gently sweetened with maple syrup, which gives it a caramel-like sweetness rather than a sugary flavour. Layered with yogurt and berries, the clusters also make a delicious dessert or after-school snack. They look really fancy yet take literally seconds to throw together!

300g / 3 cups rolled oats

100g / ½ cup buckwheat (p10)

30g / 4 TBSP cocoa powder

30g / 3 TBSP coconut sugar or unrefined cane sugar

¼ tsp salt

75g / ½ cup hazelnuts, roughly chopped

65g / ½ cup pecans, roughly chopped

70g / ½ cup dried cranberries (preferably sweetened with fruit juice)

150ml / ½ cup maple syrup

2 tsp vanilla extract

45g / 3 TBSP virgin coconut oil, melted

1   Preheat the oven to 150C (130C fan) / 300F. Line a large baking tray (38 x 26cm / 15 x 10 inches) with non-stick baking paper. If your coconut oil is solid, place in the oven in a heat-proof bowl for a couple of minutes until it has liquefied. Be careful when removing the bowl as it will be very hot!

2   In a large mixing bowl, stir together the oats, buckwheat, cocoa powder, sugar and salt. Stir in the nuts. You can also stir in the cranberries at this stage or, if you'd like to preserve their vibrant colour and nutrients, add them to the granola once it's baked.

3   Pour in the maple syrup and vanilla extract, and stir until all the grains become coated and shiny. Add the coconut oil and stir until thoroughly combined. Spread the granola out evenly on the prepared baking tray. Press down firmly with a silicone spatula so that the mixture sticks together as if you were making a thin granola bar.

4   Bake for 40 minutes. Remove from the oven and leave to cool. (The granola will firm up as it cools). Once completely cooled, break up the granola. The clusters from the centre of the tray may still feel a little soft when fresh baked, but I find they firm up and become crunchy over time. Stored in an airtight container in a cool place, the granola will last for weeks.

THE GOOD STUFF ♥

Rich in protein and dietary fibre, oats provide slow release energy and help balance blood sugar levels. Eaten on a regular basis, they promote cardiovascular health and can help to lower cholesterol levels. They are a rich source of B vitamins and minerals including magnesium, zinc and iron. Just ½ cup of oats provides 20% of the recommended daily amount of iron.

Creamy Overnight Oats

Serves: 1   Hands on : 2 minutes   Ready in: 12 minutes

In the warmer months, porridge gets switched in our house for a bowl of delicious overnight oats. Infused in milk and natural yogurt, the oats become soft and super creamy. Sprinkle on your favourite toppings and pop the oats in the refrigerator. In the morning, your breakfast will be ready and waiting for you. All that's left to do is grab a spoon and dive right in. Oats prepared in a mason or kilner jar make a great breakfast 'on the go'.

50g / ½ cup rolled oats
pinch of ground cinnamon

120ml / ½ cup non-dairy milk
4 TBSP natural non-dairy yogurt
Pick 'n' Mix toppings (p24)

1   Add the oats to a jar and sprinkle on the cinnamon.

2   Stir in the milk and yogurt.

3   Sprinkle on your chosen toppings, cover with a lid, and chill in the refrigerator overnight.

Chocolate Overnight Oats

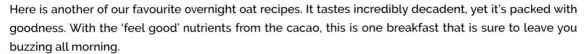

Serves: 1   Hands on : 2 minutes   Ready in: 12 minutes

Here is another of our favourite overnight oat recipes. It tastes incredibly decadent, yet it's packed with goodness. With the 'feel good' nutrients from the cacao, this is one breakfast that is sure to leave you buzzing all morning.

50g / ½ cup rolled oats
1 TBSP cacao or cocoa powder

180ml / ¾ cup non-dairy milk
½ TBSP maple syrup, or to taste
Pick 'n' Mix toppings (p24)

1   Stir together the oats and cacao/cocoa powder.

2   Stir in the milk and maple syrup.

3   Sprinkle on your chosen toppings, cover with a lid, and chill in the refrigerator overnight.

TIP Did you forget to soak your oats overnight? No worries. Soak quick oats for 5-10 minutes in the morning and they'll be soft enough to eat.

Swiss-Style Muesli

Serves: 1   Hands on: 5 minutes   Ready in: 10 minutes

When it comes to muesli, everyone has their own specific tastes. Some people like it nutty, others like it fruity. By using our Pick 'n' Mix jars, you can tailor your muesli bowl to suit your own individual tastes. You can also switch it up and have a different combination every day. Muesli will never be boring again.

50g / ½ cup rolled oats
pinch of ground cinnamon
freshly squeezed juice from one juicy orange

125g / ½ cup non-dairy natural yogurt
Pick 'n' Mix toppings (p24)

1   Place the oats and cinnamon in a bowl. Pour in the orange juice and stir to combine. Set aside for 5-10 minutes, until the oats have softened. (You can leave the oats to soak overnight but use jumbo oats as they hold their shape better).

2   Stir in the yogurt. Add a selection of chopped nuts, seeds and dried fruits and serve.

Banana Ice Cream Breakfast Bowl

Serves: 1   Hands on: 5 minutes   Ready in: 5 minutes

In the warmer months, nothing beats a cooling bowl of banana ice cream for breakfast. It might sound a bit naughty to eat ice cream for breakfast, but this bowl is filled with nothing but goodness. The base is a blend of frozen banana, mango and milk that magically transforms into the creamiest, smoothest soft serve. Adding some chia seeds and almond butter into the blend gives a boost of protein and omega 3, and will leave you feeling full up for hours.

180ml / ¾ cup non-dairy milk
1½ very ripe frozen peeled bananas (170g)
85g / heaping ½ cup frozen mango chunks
pinch of ground cinnamon
1 TBSP chia seeds
1 TBSP almond butter, optional

Suggested toppings:
fresh or frozen berries
toasted flaked almonds
toasted coconut chips
chopped walnuts or pecans

1   Slice the bananas into coins.

2   - In a power blender: Pour the milk into the jug, followed by the banana, mango, cinnamon, chia seeds and optional almond butter. Using a tamper tool, push the ingredients onto the blade and blend from low to high speed until completely smooth. Add a splash more milk, if needed, to get things moving.

- Or in a food processor: Add all the ingredients and process for a couple of minutes, until smooth. Stop now and then to redistribute the fruit around the bowl.

3   Scoop the mixture into a breakfast bowl. (If your house is very warm, chill the bowl in the freezer for 5 minutes prior to serving). Top with your favourite berries and nuts, then tuck in. If you're going to hold the bowl, wrap a tea cloth around it to prevent the heat of your hands melting the ice cream.

Chocolate Banana Energy Smoothie

Serves: 1-2   Hands on: 5 minutes   Ready in: 5 minutes

This 'breakfast in a glass' is perfect for those mornings when you're in a rush or haven't got an appetite for cereal. It's creamy, chocolatey and tastes decadent. It also happens to be packed with nutrients, including antioxidants, B vitamins and minerals. The addition of chia seeds, almonds and oats provides slow release energy and will leave you feeling full for hours. This smoothie also makes a delicious after-school snack and post-exercise recovery drink.

240ml / 1 cup non-dairy milk
1 very ripe frozen peeled banana
1 TBSP cacao or cocoa powder
1 TBSP chia seeds

1 TBSP almond butter
1 tsp maple syrup, or to taste
2 TBSP rolled oats (quick oats not jumbo), optional

1   Slice the banana into coins.

2   Place all the ingredients in a high speed blender. Blend for a couple of minutes until smooth. Taste test and add a touch more milk or sweetener, if needed.

Friendly Green Monster Smoothie

Serves 1-2   Hands on: 5 minutes   Ready in: 5 minutes

You might have noticed that there is a craze at the moment for green breakfast smoothies, fondly referred to as the 'Green Monster' movement. Adding a handful of leafy greens helps to alkalise your breakfast, which makes for happy, healthy tummies. Plus the day has only just started and you've already eaten one of your daily portions of greens. How great does that feel?

If you're new to green smoothies, I would recommend starting with our Friendly Green Monster. It's sweet and flavourful, and the spinach is not detectable in the slightest. Plus it's a delicate light green (rather than scary green!) If you've got kids, this is a great way to encourage them to enjoy their greens - just don't reveal the secret ingredient until they've given you the big thumbs up. Sneaky I know, but it works!

240ml / 1 cup soya or almond milk

1 small-medium organic sweet apple (e.g. Gala), cored and chopped

1 small very ripe frozen peeled banana, sliced into coins

1 handful of fresh spinach leaves

1 TBSP almond butter

1 TBSP chia seeds

maple syrup, optional

1   Place all the ingredients in a high speed blender and blend smooth. Add a touch more milk or sweetener, if desired.

Blueberry Vanilla Chia Pudding

Serves: 2   Hands on: 6 minutes   Ready in: 6-36 minutes

Dessert for breakfast anyone? This creamy pudding is packed with nutrient-rich ingredients that provide slow release energy and keep you feeling full for hours. What a great way to start the day! You can easily make it the night before and store it in the refrigerator for a fast 'grab and go' breakfast. We also love to serve this pudding as a quick weekday dessert.

240ml / 1 cup non-dairy milk
3 TBSP chia seeds
40g / ¼ cup raw cashews
¾ tsp vanilla extract
2 soft, sticky dates (e.g. Medjool), pitted
pinch of salt

70g / ½ cup frozen blueberries
maple syrup, optional

Suggested toppings:
Goji Nut Sprinkles (p37)
Granola (p27)

1   If you don't have a power blender, first soften the cashews by soaking in freshly boiled water for 30 minutes. 5 minutes before the end of the soaking time, add the dates. Drain thoroughly.

2   Place all the ingredients in a high speed blender, starting with the milk. Give the ingredients a stir so that they are coated in milk. Start blending on low speed to break up the nuts and dates, then blend on high speed for a couple of minutes until completely smooth. Stop now and then to scrape down the sides. Taste test and add a splash of maple syrup, if desired.

3   Scoop into two small bowls or ramekins and sprinkle on your desired toppings. The puddings can either be served immediately or chilled in the refrigerator for up to 24 hours. If storing in the refrigerator, cover the bowls to make them airtight. This will ensure the puddings keep their vibrant purple colour.

Goji Nut Sprinkles

Makes: 10 servings   Hands on: 5 minutes   Ready in: 5 minutes

These sprinkles come in handy when you need a quick topping to 'dress up' a breakfast or dessert. They're especially suited for children as the pieces are broken up nice and small.

4 TBSP toasted coconut chips

4 TBSP toasted flaked almonds

2 TBSP pecans

4 TBSP dried goji berries

1   Place the coconut chips, pecans and 2 TBSP of the almonds in a bowl and crush them between your fingers to break them up.

2   Add the remaining 2 TBSP of almonds and the goji berries to a mini food processor and whiz into crumbs (I use the bowl attachment that came with my hand blender).

3   Combine all the ingredients and transfer to an airtight jar. Store in the refrigerator where they will keep for weeks.

Easy Vegan Blender Pancakes

Serves: 2-3 Hands on: 20-35 minutes Ready in: 20-35 minutes

Sunday mornings typically start in our house with a session of pancake making. Our 'go to' recipe is this blend of whole grains and fruit, which we love to top with a sprinkling of crunchy nuts, ground linseed and maple syrup. These pancakes are incredibly easy to make. It's simply a case of whizzing all the ingredients together, then pouring and frying. It's another great recipe to get the kids involved in.

1 very ripe medium banana or 1 small-medium sweet organic apple (e.g. Gala)

240ml / 1 cup sweetened soya milk (see Tip below)

70g / ½ cup wholemeal (whole wheat pastry) flour, chapatti flour or GF flour mix

35g / ⅓ cup rolled oats (quick oats, not jumbo)

1½ tsp baking powder

½ tsp ground cinnamon

1 tsp vanilla extract

pinch of salt

½ TBSP organic rapeseed (canola) oil or other neutral-flavoured oil, for frying

Suggested toppings:
chopped pecans and walnuts

ground linseed (flaxseed)

maple syrup

1   Peel and slice a banana, or core and chop an apple (no need to peel the apple).

2   Blend the milk and banana/apple until smooth, either using a jug blender or tall jug and hand blender. Add the flour, oats, baking powder, cinnamon, vanilla extract and salt, and blend until incorporated.

3   If possible, use two non-stick frying pans (skillets) to halve the cooking time. Brush the bottom of the pan with a little oil and preheat on medium heat. To check the pan is hot enough, flick some drops of water into the pan. If it sizzles, it's ready.

4   Pour ¼ cup of batter into the pan. Once the pancake starts to firm up, carefully flip it over using a slotted turner. Cook for a further minute or so, until the underneath is browned. Place the pancake in a warm oven while you prepare the rest.

5   Any leftover pancakes can be stored in the refrigerator for up to three days. Gently warm through in a frying pan (skillet) before serving.

TIP I've found soya milk to be the best milk for pancake making as it produces robust pancakes that are easy to flip over. For these Easy Vegan Blender Pancakes, the soya milk cannot be substituted with other types of non-dairy milk. They just don't work as well.

THE GOOD STUFF ♥

Walnuts are one of the most nutrient-dense
nuts. They are packed with antioxidant and
anti-inflammatory phytonutrients, minerals
and B vitamins. They are also a rich source
of omega 3 essential fatty acids.

Crêpe-Style Pancakes

Serves: 3   Hands on: 20-26 minutes   Ready in: 20-26 minutes

These crêpe-style pancakes make a lovely treat for weekend breakfasts. They are also perfect for Shrove Tuesday, served with a squeeze of lemon juice and sprinkling of sugar. Coconut sugar is especially good!

Dry ingredients

110g / ¾ cup plain (all purpose) flour

70g / ½ cup fine wholemeal (whole wheat pastry) flour or chapatti flour

1 tsp baking powder

¼ tsp salt

Wet ingredients

240ml / 1 cup soya milk (see Tip below)

160ml / ⅔ cup water

1 TBSP organic rapeseed (canola) oil (or other neutral-flavoured oil), plus extra for frying

1 TBSP maple syrup

1 tsp vanilla extract

Suggested fillings:

freshly squeezed lemon juice and a sprinkling of unrefined sugar

chocolate sauce (recipe overleaf), banana slices, sprinkling of finely chopped walnuts

1   Sift the dry ingredients into a large bowl, preferably one with a pouring spout. Tip any remaining wheatgerm from the sieve into the bowl. Make a well in the middle and pour in the wet ingredients. Whisk to combine. Add a little more milk, if needed, to make a thin, pourable batter.

2   If possible, use two large non-stick frying pans (skillets) to halve the cooking time. Brush the bottom of the pan with oil and preheat on medium high. To check it's hot enough, flick some drops of water into the pan. If the water sizzles, it's ready.

3   Pour ⅓ cup of batter into the centre of the pan and swirl to thin out. Leave the pancake to firm up. When the underside is lightly browned (about 1½ minutes), loosen the edges using a slotted turner then flip over. Cook for a further 30 seconds or so, until the second side is browned. Transfer to a warm oven while you cook the remaining pancakes.

4   Add your favourite toppings and serve. Any leftover pancakes can be stored in the refrigerator for up to three days. Gently heat through before serving.

TIP The batter can be made up to 24 hours in advance and stored in the refrigerator. It may thicken up over time, so whisk in a splash more milk before cooking. Soya milk is our preferred milk for these Crêpe-Style Pancakes as the batter doesn't require resting time. It also makes robust pancakes that are easy to flip over. For this recipe, I don't recommend substituting the soya milk with other types of non-dairy milk.

Chocolate Sauce

Yield: about 160ml / 1/2 cup   Hands on: 7 minutes   Ready in: 7 minutes

This home-made chocolate sauce is perfect for drizzling on pancakes, waffles and ice cream. If you love the nut-chocolate combo, whisk in some nut butter or ground almonds. As well as enhancing the flavour and texture, the nuts give the sauce a great nutrient boost.

120ml / ½ cup non-dairy milk
2 TBSP sieved cocoa powder
3 TBSP maple syrup
1 tsp vanilla extract
2 tsp cornflour (cornstarch), dissolved in 1 TBSP water

Optional add-ins:
1 TBSP almond butter (or other nut butter)
4 TBSP ground almonds

1   Place all the ingredients in a small saucepan and whisk to combine. Bring to the boil, then reduce the heat and simmer gently, whisking regularly. When the sauce has thickened to the desired consistency, remove from the heat.

2   The sauce can be stored in the refrigerator for up to five days. It may thicken over time, so whisk in a little extra milk before serving.

Easy Vegan Waffles

Serves: 3   Hands on: 20 minutes   Ready in: 20 minutes

Unlike traditional waffles which are filled with cow's milk, eggs, butter, white flour and sugar, this version is fat free and packed with healthful, nutrition-rich ingredients like banana, whole grain flour and oats. We love to serve them as a weekend breakfast. They also make a tasty after-school snack and have proven to be a big hit with Lil' L and his friends.

1 very ripe medium banana, sliced

180ml / ¾ cup soya or almond milk

140g / 1 cup fine wholemeal (whole wheat pastry) flour, chapatti flour or GF flour mix

50g / ½ cup rolled oats (quick oats, not jumbo)

1 tsp baking powder

½ tsp ground cinnamon

¼ tsp salt

40ml / 2 TBSP maple syrup

coconut oil (or oil of choice), for greasing

Suggested toppings:

maple syrup

chopped walnuts, pecans or almonds

fresh or frozen berries

1   Place the banana and milk in a large bowl and blend smooth using a hand blender (alternatively use a jug blender).

2   Add the flour, oats, baking powder, cinnamon, salt and maple syrup. Blend to combine. The batter should be very thick, but pourable. Add a touch more milk if needed, to attain the desired consistency. (If you're using GF flour, you may need up to 4 TBSP of extra liquid).

3   Leave the batter to rest for a few minutes (this can happen while the waffle maker heats up).

4   When the waffle maker is hot, brush with oil using a silicone pastry brush. Consult your waffle maker instructions for the quantity of batter to use. I have a quad waffle maker and scoop two slightly rounded tablespoons into each quad.

5   Cook the waffles until they are golden brown all over (4-7 minutes depending on your waffle maker). Transfer to a wire cooling rack while you prepare the remaining waffles.

6   Add your chosen toppings and serve. Any leftover waffles can be stored in the refrigerator for up to three days. Heat them through in the toaster or under the grill (broiler) before serving.

Carrot Cake Waffles

Serves: 3-4   Hands on: 30 minutes   Ready in: 30 minutes

Inspired by one of my all-time favourite cakes, these waffles are filled with sweet warming spices and a hint of coconut. They even include a carrot, though you'd never detect it!

180ml / ¾ cup soya or almond milk

90g / 1 cup carrot, finely grated

1 small-medium sweet organic apple (e.g. Gala), cored and chopped (no need to peel)

40ml / 2 TBSP maple syrup

40ml / 2 TBSP black treacle (molasses) or Blackstrap molasses

140g / 1 cup fine wholemeal (whole wheat pastry) flour, chapatti flour or GF flour mix

50g / ½ cup rolled oats (quick oats, not jumbo)

1 tsp baking powder

2 tsp ground cinnamon

pinch of ground nutmeg

¼ tsp salt

10g / 2 TBSP desiccated coconut

coconut oil (or oil of choice), for greasing

Suggested toppings:

Coconut 'Clotted Cream' (recipe overleaf), Chocolate Sauce (p41) or maple syrup

chopped walnuts and pecans

1   Add the milk, carrot, apple, syrup and molasses to a large bowl and whiz smooth with a hand blender.

2   Add the flour, oats, baking powder, cinnamon, nutmeg and salt to the bowl. Blend until fully combined. Add the desiccated coconut and pulse a few times to combine. The batter should be very thick, but pourable. Add a splash more milk, if needed, to attain the desired consistency. (If you're using GF flour, you may need up to 4 TBSP extra milk).

3   Leave the batter to rest while the waffle maker heats up.

4   When the waffle maker is hot, brush the plates with oil using a silicone pastry brush. Consult the manufacturer's instructions for the quantity of batter to use. (I have a quad waffle maker and scoop two heaped tablespoons into each quad).

5   Cook the waffles until they are lightly browned all over (4-7 minutes, depending on your waffle maker). Transfer to a wire cooling rack while you prepare the remaining waffles.

6   Add your chosen toppings and serve. The waffles are best served fresh, but any leftover waffles can be stored in the refrigerator for up to three days. Heat through in the toaster or under the grill (broiler) before serving.

TIP The apple can be substituted with one very ripe small-medium banana. You can even use frozen banana. Simply slice into coins and leave to thaw slightly before blending. Since the batter will be colder, the waffles may take a minute or two extra to cook.

Coconut 'Clotted Cream'

Yield: about 160g / 1 cup   Hands on: 5 minutes   Ready in: 5 minutes (+ 24 hours chilling)

Lightly sweetened and with a hint of vanilla, this spreadable coconut cream makes a delicious alternative to dairy clotted cream. We love it as a topping for our Carrot Cake Waffles (recipe overleaf). It's also perfect for serving as part of a dairy-free English Cream Tea (p46) or the quintessentially English dessert 'Strawberries and Cream'.

250ml / 8½ fl oz coconut cream

1 TBSP icing (powdered) sugar
½ tsp vanilla extract

1   Place the coconut cream in the refrigerator at least 24 hours in advance (this helps the cream to separate from the water). Being careful not to shake it, open the container and scoop the solid coconut cream into a measuring jug (you can discard the water). If your house is very warm, first chill the jug in the freezer for a few minutes.

2   Use a fork to break up the coconut cream then beat using an electric hand mixer until smooth.

3   Sieve in the powdered sugar. Add the vanilla extract and beat to combine. Taste test and add a touch more sweetener, if desired.

4   Chill until ready to serve. This cream will keep up to a week in the refrigerator. It may firm up over time, so whisk with a fork, if needed, before serving.

English Scones

Makes: 9 large scones   Hands on: 20 minutes   Ready in: 35 minutes

Warm, freshly baked scones make a wonderful weekend breakfast. We love to serve them filled with a sweet-tasting strawberry spread, such as the one made by St Dalfour. Add Coconut 'Clotted Cream' (p45) and a pot of tea for a delicious dairy-free version of the classic English Cream Tea, perfect for serving at 'elevenses' or afternoon tea parties.

300ml / 1¼ cups soya milk

10ml / 2 tsp apple cider vinegar

270g / 2 cups plain (all purpose) flour

270g / 2 cups fine wholemeal (whole wheat pastry) flour or chapatti flour

20g / 4 tsp baking powder

¼ tsp salt

90g / 6 TBSP dairy-free spread/vegan butter

36g / 3 TBSP unrefined cane sugar

80g / ½ cup raisins, optional

soya milk, for glaze

Filling

Coconut 'Clotted Cream' (p45) or dairy-free spread/vegan butter

strawberry jam or fruit spread (e.g. St Dalfour)

1 Preheat the oven to 220C (200C fan) / 425F. Line a large baking tray with non-stick baking paper.

2 Whisk together the milk and vinegar in a jug and set to one side.

3 Place the flours, baking powder and salt in a large bowl and stir through to combine. Using your finger tips, rub in the dairy-free spread/vegan butter until fully incorporated. Mix in the sugar and raisins.

4 Make a well in the centre and pour in three quarters of the milk and vinegar mixture. Stir to combine. Add the remaining liquid a little at a time, while using your hands to bring the mixture together into a soft, slightly sticky dough. Depending on the type of flour you use, you may not need all the milk. Do not overwork the mixture, as this will result in heavy scones.

5 Turn out the dough onto a lightly floured surface. Sprinkle a little flour on top and gently roll out to a thickness of 2.5cm / 1 inch. Cut out the dough using a 7.5cm / 3 inch metal pastry cutter. Press down swiftly on the cutter, lift straight up and push out the dough onto the prepared tray. Do not twist the cutter as you press down otherwise you will end up with funny shaped scones. Repeat until all the dough is used up, re-rolling the scraps as needed.

6 Brush the tops of the scones with soya milk, for a golden glaze.

7 Bake the scones in the preheated oven for 15 minutes, until the tops and bottoms are lightly browned. Leave to cool slightly before serving.

8 These scones are best served fresh, but will last a couple of days in an airtight container. They also freeze well.

Apple Cinnamon Monkey Bread

Serves: 3   Hands on: 20-30 minutes   Ready in: 2 hours

Monkey Bread (aka Bubbleloaf) are warm sweet dough balls that make the most delicious weekend breakfast or 'elevenses'. It's typically made with lots of refined sugar, butter and flour, but we make a healthier version using whole grains and fruit. This recipe has been a big hit with my blog readers' families. It's a great one to get the kids involved in making too.

TIP To save time in the morning, the dough can be prepared the night before, covered in cling film (plastic wrap) and chilled in the refrigerator. In the morning, remove the dough about 20 minutes before you need to use it.

Dough

165g / 1¼ cups fine wholemeal (whole wheat pastry) flour or chapatti flour

140g / 1 cup plain (all purpose) flour

½ tsp fast action yeast

½ tsp salt

1 TBSP coconut sugar or unrefined cane sugar

170ml / ¾ cup lukewarm water

1 TBSP extra virgin olive oil

Apple cinnamon syrup

2 small sweet organic apples (220g) or 190g / ¾ cup apple sauce

30g / 2 TBSP virgin coconut oil

40ml / 2 TBSP maple syrup

1 TBSP coconut sugar or unrefined cane sugar

1 tsp ground cinnamon

Cinnamon sugar

1 TBSP coconut sugar or unrefined cane sugar

1 tsp ground cinnamon

1   Prepare the dough:

- In a bread maker: Tip all the ingredients in the pan and select 'pizza dough'. The programme should take around 45 minutes. When it signals that it's ready, leave the dough to rest in the machine for a further 15 minutes or so.

- Or by hand: Place the flours, yeast, salt and sugar in a large bowl. Stir in the warm water and oil using a spoon, then bring it together with your hands to form a sticky dough. Knead for 10 minutes, until the dough is smooth. Place in a lightly oiled bowl, cover with a damp tea cloth and leave in a warm place for an hour to prove.

2   Once the dough is ready, prepare the apple cinnamon syrup. Core the apples and chop into pieces. Place them in a bowl and blitz into a purée using a hand blender. Place the apple purée, coconut oil, syrup, sugar and cinnamon in a pan and gently heat until the oil has melted. Stir through, then remove from the heat.

3   To make the cinnamon sugar, combine 1 TBSP sugar and 1 tsp ground cinnamon in a small container.

4   Preheat the oven to 200C (180C fan) / 400F. Grease a 23cm / 9 inch baking pan with oil.

5   Prepare the dough balls: Pull off a small amount of dough and roll into a ball about 2.5cm / 1 inch in diameter. Place the ball in the prepared tin. Repeat until all the dough has been used. Space out the balls in the pan (they will expand as they cook). Spoon the apple cinnamon syrup between the balls and round the edges of the pan. Sprinkle the cinnamon sugar on top.

6   Bake in the preheated oven for 25 minutes, or until the dough balls are crusty on top. Leave the pan to cool slightly, then place it in the centre of the table and invite everyone to tuck in.

7   Should there be any leftovers, store in the refrigerator for up to three days and gently warm through in the oven before serving.

Soups

Soups are incredibly easy and quick to prepare. They're also a great way to encourage children to eat veggies that they wouldn't normally even try. I tend to make one large batch of soup a week, which we enjoy as a hearty weekend lunch or light evening meal. The leftovers are perfect for quick weekday lunches at home or packed into a flask for school and work.

Tomato & Red Lentil Soup

Serves: 4   Hands on: 15 minutes   Ready in: 45 minutes

Packed with antioxidants, vitamins and minerals, this soup is a fantastic immunity-booster. With the addition of lentils, the soup also provides a healthy dose of protein, fibre and slow release energy. Hearty and filling, this soup is suitable as both a lunch and main meal option. We love to serve it with a side plate of Quick Crispy Garlic Bread (p55).

1 TBSP olive oil

1 medium onion (130g), finely diced

2-3 garlic cloves, minced

2 medium carrots (150g), quartered lengthwise and thinly sliced

1 celery stick (65g), finely diced

140g / ¾ cup red lentils, rinsed and drained

840ml / 3½ cups vegetable stock (broth)

400g / 14 oz can chopped tomatoes

3 TBSP tomato purée (paste) or sun-dried tomato paste

handful of fresh basil leaves, chopped

2 tsp unrefined sugar

salt and ground black pepper, to taste

basil or parsley leaves, for garnish

1   Gently heat the oil in a large saucepan. Add the onion, garlic, carrot and celery. Stir through, cover with a lid and leave to sweat on low heat for 5 minutes or so.

2   Meanwhile, place the lentils in a fine mesh sieve and wash under cold running water until the water runs clear.

3   Add the lentils, vegetable stock, chopped tomatoes, tomato purée, basil and sugar to the pan. Bring to the boil then reduce the heat, cover with a lid, and simmer for 20 minutes or until the lentils are tender.

4   Allow to cool slightly then transfer half of the soup to a jug blender and blend smooth. (Alternatively you can blend all the soup smooth, if you prefer). Return the soup to the pan and gently heat through. Season with salt and ground black pepper to taste.

5   Ladle into warm bowls, add the garnish and serve. Any leftovers will keep for up to five days stored in an airtight container in the refrigerator. This soup also freezes well.

Mexican Black Bean Soup

Serves: 4-6   Hand on: 15 minutes   Ready in: 45 minutes

The black bean (aka turtle bean) has a beautiful smoky flavour, which makes it perfect for adding to home-cooked Mexican dishes. Here in the UK, however, this bean tends to get neglected in favour of its big red brother, the kidney bean. I think it's high time we gave this little bean the recognition it deserves. One of my favourite ways to serve black beans is in this richly flavoured soup accompanied by some home-made cornbread (p54) or toasted tortilla chips (p53).

1 TBSP olive oil

1 medium onion (130g), finely diced

2-3 garlic cloves, minced

1 large carrot (140g), finely diced

1 large sweet potato (370g), peeled and diced

1 tsp ground cumin

1 tsp paprika (sweet or smoked)

1 tsp dried oregano

½ tsp chilli powder (use mild chilli for children)

145g / 1 cup canned or frozen sweetcorn

400g / 14 oz can chopped tomatoes

600ml / 2½ cups vegetable stock (broth)

2 x 400g / 14 oz can black beans, rinsed and drained

salt, to taste

cayenne pepper, to taste

2 TBSP nutritional yeast flakes, optional (adds savouriness and extra nutrients)

Garnish
fresh coriander leaves (cilantro)
red pepper or chilli, finely diced

1   Gently heat the oil in a large saucepan. Add the onion, garlic, carrot, sweet potato, cumin, paprika, oregano and chilli powder. Stir to combine, then cover with a lid and leave to sweat on low heat for 5 minutes.

2   Add the sweetcorn, tomatoes and stock to the pan. Bring to the boil then reduce the heat, partially cover with a lid, and simmer for 20 minutes. When the vegetables are tender, stir in the beans.

3   Remove half of the soup from the pan. Allow to cool slightly, then blend smooth in a jug blender. Return it to the pan and gently heat through. (Small children may prefer their soup completely smooth. In this case, simply add more soup to the blender).

4   Season the soup with salt, to taste. If you'd like to give the soup a spicy kick, first remove any children's portions then add a pinch of cayenne pepper.

5   Allow to cool slightly, then stir in the nutritional yeast (this helps to preserve its nutrients).

6   This soup will keep for three days in the refrigerator. It may thicken over time, so simply add a touch more water or vegetable stock. It also freezes well.

Toasted Tortilla Chips

Serves: 4   Hands on: 5 minutes   Ready in: 5-10 minutes

These crispy tortilla chips are so simple to make, and they are far more healthy than store-bought chips. If you wish, you can spice them up by sprinkling on some paprika, chilli or cumin before toasting. These chips make a great accompaniment to Mexican dishes. They also make a great snack, topped with hummus or mashed avocado and salsa.

2 large or 4 small whole grain soft tortillas (use GF tortillas, if needed)

Baking method - Preheat the oven to 190C (170C fan) / 375F. Slice the tortillas into segments and place them on two baking sheets. Bake for 8-10 minutes, or until lightly browned all over. Watch closely towards the end of the cooking time as they can burn quickly. As they cool, the tortillas will crisp up. Stored in an airtight container, they will keep for a couple of weeks.

Grill method – Place the tortillas under the grill (broiler). Keep a watch on them and, as soon as they start to brown, turn them over. When lightly browned on both sides, remove from the grill and immediately slice into segments.

Cornbread

Serves: 4-6   Hands on: 15 minutes   Ready in: 60 minutes

This fluffy, moist bread makes a great accompaniment to Mexican dishes like Black Bean Soup (p52) and Rainbow Veggie Chilli (p128). It's most delicious served warm, either fresh from the oven or sliced into thin wedges and heated through in a frying pan (skillet).

480ml / 2 cups soya milk

2 tsp apple cider vinegar

140g / 1 cup fine yellow cornmeal

140g / 1 cup fine wholemeal (whole wheat pastry) flour or chapatti flour

1½ tsp baking powder

½ tsp bicarbonate of soda (baking soda)

1 tsp salt

50ml / ¼ cup organic rapeseed (canola) oil or other neutral-flavoured oil

1 TBSP maple syrup

1   Preheat the oven to 180C (160C fan) / 350F. Grease the sides of a 20cm / 8 inch square baking pan and line the bottom with non-stick baking paper.

2   Whisk together the milk and vinegar in a large mixing bowl and set to one side for a couple of minutes.

3   Place the cornmeal, flour, baking powder, bicarbonate of soda and salt in another bowl and stir to combine.

4   Whisk the oil and syrup into the milk and vinegar.

5   Sieve the dry ingredients into the wet ingredient bowl roughly in thirds, whisking each time until smooth before adding the next third. Stir in any remaining wheatgerm from the sieve.

6   Pour the mixture into the prepared pan and bake for 30 minutes, or until a skewer inserted into the middle comes out clean.

7   Leave to cool for 15 minutes. Run a knife round the edge to loosen the bread, then invert onto a chopping board. Peel off the baking paper, then slice the bread into squares.

8   Stored in an airtight container, this bread will keep for up to five days in the refrigerator or for weeks in the freezer. Warm through before serving.

Garden Pea Soup
with Ginger & Oregano

Serves: 4   Hand on: 10 minutes   Ready in: 35 minutes

Light, fresh and sweet-tasting, garden peas are just perfect for the spring/summer seasons. However, I must admit that it took me a few years to find a pea dish that Lil' L actually liked. One of my favourites - Pea and Fresh Mint Soup - was deemed 'too peay' and 'too minty'. Inspired by an Austrian blogging friend, I thought I'd try to win him over with a creamy pea soup. I watched with trepidation as he took the first mouthful. Soon the bowl was finished and he was asking for another! As he finished off the second bowl, I decided to own up and tell him what was in the soup. He paused, then gave me 'the look', the one that says 'you tricked me'. No trickery here, you liked peas all along. We just needed this recipe to prove it.

1 TBSP olive oil
1 medium onion (130g), diced
18g root ginger (1 inch piece), finely grated
700ml / 3 cups vegetable stock (broth)
540g / 4 cups frozen green peas

1 TBSP dried oregano
120ml / ½ cup unsweetened non-dairy milk
salt and ground black pepper, to taste
parsley leaves, for garnish

1   Heat the oil in a saucepan and cook the onion on medium heat for 4 minutes.

2   Add the ginger to the pan and stir fry for a minute.

3   Add the stock, peas and oregano. Bring to the boil, then reduce the heat, cover with a lid and simmer for 15 minutes.

4   Allow the soup to cool slightly before adding the milk and blending smooth. Season with salt and pepper, to taste. Gently heat through before serving.

5   We love to serve the soup with a slice or two of Quick Crispy Garlic Bread (recipe below). Any leftover soup will keep for five days in the refrigerator.

Quick Crispy Garlic Bread

In a small bowl, mix together 1 TBSP olive oil and 1 minced garlic clove. Leave to infuse for a minute or so. Brush the oil on both sides of slices of bread using a silicone pastry brush. Fry in a hot griddle pan or frying pan (skillet) until golden brown. Press the bread into the pan using a slotted turner or spatula (this will help it brown all over). Top up the oil as needed.

Watercress Soup

Serves: 4   Hands on: 10 minutes   Ready in: 40 minutes

Raw watercress has a strong peppery taste, yet in soup it takes on a beautiful, mild flavour that even children will love. This was one of the first soups I made for Lil' L when he was a toddler and he loved it so much that he started to request it every weekend! To this day, it remains a family favourite. It's simple to make, delicious and packed with goodness.

1 TBSP olive oil

2 medium onions (280g), diced

2-3 garlic cloves, minced

2-3 medium potatoes (420g), diced (no need to peel if you have a high speed blender)

150g / 3 packed cups watercress

800ml / 3½ cups vegetable stock (broth)

salt, to taste

handful each of toasted pumpkin, sunflower and sesame seeds, for garnish

1   Gently heat the oil in a large saucepan. Add the onion, garlic, potatoes and watercress. Cover with a lid and sweat on low heat for 10 minutes, stirring occasionally.

2   Add the stock, bring to the boil then reduce the heat, cover with a lid, and simmer for 15 minutes or until the potato is soft. Allow to cool slightly before blending smooth. Season with salt, to taste.

3   Toast the seeds in a frying pan (skillet) on medium heat, either dry or with a splash of olive oil. Stir continuously and as soon as the seeds start to brown, remove from the heat.

4   When ready to serve, gently heat the soup. Ladle into warm bowls and garnish with toasted seeds. Any leftovers will keep in the refrigerator for up to five days.

THE GOOD STUFF ♥

Watercress has powerful antioxidant and anti-inflammatory properties, and is especially rich in vitamin C, vitamin K, betacarotene, lutein and zeaxanthin. It is also a rich source of chlorophyll, a dark green pigment, which promotes healthy blood cells and boosts circulation.

Indian-Spiced Creamy Parsnip Soup

Serves: 4   Hands on: 20 minutes   Ready in: 40 minutes

When autumn is almost over and the weather is starting to turn cold, we like to wrap up warm, pour ourselves a steaming mug of parsnip soup, and head outside to enjoy the last opportunities for al fresco dining. This soup is thick, creamy and spiced, making it a wonderful winter warmer. I've kept it mild enough for children (and spice wimps like me), but feel free to crank up the heat by adding more garam masala.

1 TBSP olive oil

1 medium onion (140g), diced

2-3 garlic cloves, minced

1 tsp garam masala (or more if you like heat)

3-4 medium parsnips (450g), sliced into thin disks*

1 medium sweet potato (160g), diced*

* No need to peel if you have a high speed blender

1 litre / 4 cups vegetable stock (broth)

50g / ¼ cup creamed coconut, finely chopped (see Tip on p120)

salt, to taste

Suggested garnish:

swirl of coconut cream

sprinkling of smoked paprika

1   Gently heat the oil in a large saucepan and cook the onion for 4 minutes.

2   Add the garlic and garam masala to the pan and cook for a further minute.

3   Add the parsnips, potato and vegetable stock. Bring to the boil then reduce the heat, cover with a lid, and simmer for 15 minutes or until the vegetables are tender.

4   Stir in the creamed coconut then remove the pan from the heat. Leave to cool slightly before blending smooth in a jug blender. Add a touch more stock or water (if needed) to reach the desired consistency.

5   Return the soup to the pan and gently heat through. Season with salt, to taste.

6   Ladle into warm bowls, add the garnish and serve. Any leftover soup will keep for five days in the refrigerator. It is also freezable.

THE GOOD STUFF ♥
Parsnips are rich in vitamin C and folate.
They are also a good source of dietary
fibre, which helps to lower cholesterol
and balance blood sugar levels.

Turmeric has long been used as a condiment and healing remedy. Its orange pigment called 'curcumin' has potent antioxidant, anti-inflammatory and disease-fighting properties. Turmeric is also rich in iron and manganese.

Malaysian Coconut Noodle Soup

Serves: 4   Hands on: 35 minutes   Ready in: 35 minutes

This is my family-friendly, plant-based version of the traditional Malaysian soup Laksa Lemak. It's beautifully fragrant, light, yet filling enough to be served as a satisfying lunch or dinner option. I've chosen to use carrots and broccoli florets in this dish for added texture, colour and nutrients, but feel free to substitute with your favourite Asian vegetables.

Spice paste

25g root ginger (2 inch piece), finely grated

2-3 garlic cloves, minced

2 lemongrass stalks, trimmed and finely sliced

1 red chilli, deseeded and finely diced*

1 small red onion (90g), finely diced

1 tsp ground coriander

½ tsp ground cumin

1½ TBSP freshly squeezed lime juice

* If serving to children, use a mild chilli and remove the inner white membrane as this is where the heat is concentrated. Alternatively, omit the chilli from the paste and add it to the soup once the children's portions have been served.

Noodle soup

400ml / 14 oz can coconut milk

½ tsp ground turmeric

2 dried kaffir lime leaves

720ml / 3 cups hot vegetable stock (broth)

1 TBSP tamari or reduced-salt soy sauce

2 tsp unrefined sugar

2 medium carrots (170g), sliced into thin disks

1 small head of broccoli (300g) sliced into 16 florets

90g / 1 cup mushrooms, sliced

200g / 7 oz smoked or marinated tofu, cubed (p19)

250g / 9 oz whole wheat or brown rice noodles

fresh coriander leaves (cilantro) and diced red chilli or bell pepper, for garnish

1   Place the spice paste ingredients in a mini food processor along with 2-3 TBSP coconut milk and blend into a smooth paste. (I use the bowl attachment that came with my hand blender).

2   Gently cook the paste in a large, heavy-bottomed pan for a couple of minutes.

3   Stir in the remaining coconut milk, turmeric and kaffir lime leaves. Bring to the boil then reduce the heat and gently simmer, uncovered, for 5 minutes.

4   Add the stock, soy sauce and sugar to the pan, along with the carrots. Simmer for 5 minutes.

5   Add the broccoli florets, mushrooms and tofu cubes, and simmer for a further 10 minutes, or until the broccoli is tender but retains a bite.

6   Meanwhile, cook the noodles as per the instructions on the packet.

7   Divide the noodles between four bowls and spoon the soup on top (discard the kaffir lime leaves). Sprinkle on the garnish, and serve immediately with chopsticks (or fork) and a spoon for the gravy.

8   Any leftover soup (excluding the noodles) can be stored in the refrigerator for up to five days. If using store-bought tofu, check the storage instructions on the packet.

Thai Sweet Potato & Coconut Soup

Serves: 4   Hands on: 20 minutes   Ready in: 40 minutes

With its beautiful golden hue and fragrant, warming spices, this has got to be the perfect soup for the autumn season. The ginger, chilli, lemongrass and kaffir lime leaves give this soup its distinct Thai flavour, but I've kept it mild enough for children. Feel free to crank up the heat by adding more chillies.

1 medium onion (130g), diced

2-3 garlic cloves, minced

18g root ginger (1 inch piece), finely grated

1 red chilli, deseeded and finely diced*

1 tsp ground cumin

1 tsp ground coriander

2-3 medium sweet potatoes (500g), diced (no need to peel if you have a high speed blender)

* If serving to children, use a mild chilli and remove the inner white membrane as this is where the heat is concentrated. Alternatively, blend in the chilli once the children's portions have been removed.

2 medium carrots (140g), thinly sliced

400ml / 14 oz can coconut milk

500ml / 2 cups vegetable stock (broth)

2 dried kaffir lime leaves

1 lemongrass stalk, bruised

50g / ¼ cup creamed coconut, finely chopped (see Tip on p120)

salt, to taste

Garnish
4 TBSP Soy Toasted Sunflower Seeds (recipe overleaf)

1   Gently heat 2-3 TBSP of the coconut milk in a large pan and fry the onion, garlic, ginger, chilli, cumin and coriander for a couple of minutes, stirring regularly.

2   Add the sweet potato and carrot along with the remaining coconut milk, vegetable stock, kaffir lime leaves and bruised lemongrass. Bring to the boil then reduce the heat, cover with a lid, and simmer for 20 minutes or until the vegetables are soft. Leave to cool slightly.

3   Discard the kaffir lime leaves and lemongrass. Transfer the soup to a jug blender and blend until silky smooth. Return the soup to the pan and gently heat through. Stir in the creamed coconut until melted. Season with salt, to taste.

4   Ladle the soup into warm bowls, sprinkle on the garnish and serve. Any leftovers can be stored in the refrigerator for up to five days. This soup also freezes well.

THE GOOD STUFF ♥

Sweet potatoes are a great source of slow release energy. They are also packed with antioxidants. Just one medium baked potato contains 438% of the vitamin A RDA and 37% of vitamin C.

Soy Toasted Sunflower Seeds

Heat a non-stick frying pan (skillet) on medium heat and fry 4 TBSP sunflower seeds in 1½ tsp soy sauce. Stir continuously until they start to brown and have dried out. Remove from the heat and tip onto a plate. If not using immediately, store in an airtight container in the refrigerator, where they will keep for weeks.

Japanese Miso Noodle Soup

Serves: 3-4 Hands on: 25 minutes Ready in: 25 minutes

With its vibrant crunchy veggies, soft chewy noodles and rich 'umami' flavour, this soup truly is a feast for the senses. It's simple to prepare and perfect for a light weekday dinner option or weekend lunch.

200g / 7 oz whole wheat noodles (or use brown rice noodles for a GF option)

1 TBSP olive oil

1 medium red onion (130g), sliced

2 garlic cloves, minced

18g root ginger (1 inch piece), finely grated

125g / 1½ cups chestnut (or crimini) mushrooms, chopped into chunks

1 small red bell pepper (150g), deseeded and sliced

12 sugar snap peas

1 litre / 4 cups vegetable stock (broth)

3 TBSP miso paste (use brown rice miso for a GF option)

1 TBSP tamari or reduced-salt soy sauce

½ tsp unrefined sugar

160g / 2 cups pak choi, shredded

200g / 7 oz smoked or marinated tofu, cubed (p19)

1 Prepare a large pan of boiling water and cook the noodles according to the instructions on the packet. Drain, refresh under cold running water, and set to one side.

2 Heat the oil in the pan and stir fry the onion, garlic and ginger for a couple of minutes. Add a splash of water if it starts to stick.

3 Add the mushrooms, bell pepper and sugar snap peas, and continue stir frying for about 5 minutes.

4 Add the vegetable stock, miso paste, soy sauce and sugar. Gently heat through until the miso dissolves. Keep the broth below boiling point to preserve the miso's nutrients.

5 Add the pak choi to the pan, along with the tofu and noodles. Once heated through, transfer to warm bowls and serve.

6 Miso soup is best eaten fresh. It can be stored in the refrigerator for a couple of days, but the vegetables will lose their vibrant colour and the noodles may break down on re-heating.

TIP Pan-fried tofu also works well in this dish (p19). Not a fan of tofu? Use edamame beans or toasted cashews instead.

THE GOOD STUFF ♥
Like other members of the cabbage family, pak choi (aka bok choy, Chinese cabbage) is packed with antioxidants. Just one cup of cooked pak choi provides 144% of the recommended daily amount of vitamin A, 74% of vitamin C and 72% of vitamin K. It is also a great source of calcium and iron.

THE GOOD STUFF ♥
Celery is packed with antioxidant and anti-inflammatory nutrients, including phenolic acids which have been shown to help protect against oxygen damage to cells and blood vessels. Celery is also a good source of dietary fibre and vitamin K. Just one cup of chopped celery provides 37% of the vitamin K RDA.

Italian Minestrone Soup

Serves: 5-6   Hands on: 20 minutes   Ready in: 40 minutes

This hearty soup is packed full of flavour and antioxidant-rich veggies that will leave you glowing from the inside out. The addition of pasta makes it filling enough to serve as a main meal. If making in advance, it is best to keep the pasta separate to prevent it soaking up all the soup liquid. When ready to serve, simply combine in a pan and gently heat through.

1 TBSP olive oil

1 large onion (170g), finely diced

2-3 garlic cloves, minced

2 celery stalks (140g), finely diced

2 medium carrots (200g), quartered lengthwise and thinly sliced

1 small courgette (zucchini) (120g), quartered lengthwise and sliced

100g / 1 cup chestnut (or crimini) mushrooms, diced

1 tsp each dried oregano, smoked paprika

½ tsp each dried sage, dried thyme

500g / 2 cups tomato passata

1 litre / 4 cups vegetable stock (broth)

2 TBSP tomato purée (paste)

2 tsp unrefined sugar

small handful of fresh basil leaves, roughly chopped (reserve some for the garnish)

2-3 bay leaves

400g / 14 oz can cannellini beans, drained

salt and ground black pepper, to taste

120g / 1 cup mini whole wheat pasta shapes (use GF pasta, if needed)

Garnish

1 avocado, diced

fresh basil leaves

1   Gently heat the oil in a large pan. Add the onion, garlic, celery, carrots, courgette, mushrooms, oregano, paprika, sage and thyme. Stir through, then cover with a lid and leave to sweat for 5 minutes.

2   Add the passata, stock, tomato purée, sugar, basil leaves and bay leaves. Bring to the boil, then reduce the heat, partially cover with a lid and simmer for 20 minutes, or until the vegetables are tender.

3   Stir in the beans. Season the soup with salt and pepper, to taste. Remove the bay leaves.

4   While the soup is simmering, cook the pasta until al dente, then drain and set to one side. When the soup is ready, stir in the pasta.

5   We love to serve this soup with some Crispy Garlic Bread (p55), warm focaccia or giant croutons. Any leftover soup can be refrigerated for up to three days. It is also freezable (without the pasta).

Lunches & Light Dinners

In this chapter, you'll find a selection of our favourite family-friendly weekend lunches and light weekday dinners. All the recipes can easily be elevated to main meal status with the addition of a side dish, such as a colourful salad, or a simple starter, like raw veggie sticks (crudités) and hummus dip.

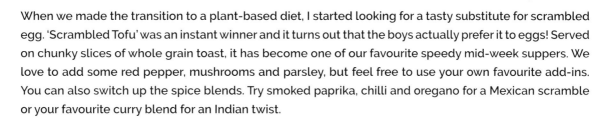

Scrambled Tofu on Toast

Serves: 4   Hands on: 20 minutes   Ready in: 20 minutes

When we made the transition to a plant-based diet, I started looking for a tasty substitute for scrambled egg. 'Scrambled Tofu' was an instant winner and it turns out that the boys actually prefer it to eggs! Served on chunky slices of whole grain toast, it has become one of our favourite speedy mid-week suppers. We love to add some red pepper, mushrooms and parsley, but feel free to use your own favourite add-ins. You can also switch up the spice blends. Try smoked paprika, chilli and oregano for a Mexican scramble or your favourite curry blend for an Indian twist.

400g / 14 oz firm tofu
½ TBSP olive oil
1 medium onion (130g), finely diced
2 garlic cloves, minced
1 red bell or sweet romano pepper, deseeded and diced
1½ -2 tsp ground cumin

½ tsp ground turmeric
1 TBSP tamari or reduced-salt soy sauce
handful of mushrooms (100g), sliced
1 TBSP parsley, finely chopped
2 TBSP nutritional yeast flakes
salt and ground black pepper, to taste

1   Drain the tofu and squeeze out as much water as possible.

2   Heat the oil in a large frying pan (skillet) on medium heat and cook the onion until it starts to soften (about 4 minutes). Meanwhile, prepare the remaining veggies.

3   Add the garlic, red pepper and cumin to the pan, and cook for a minute or so.

4   Crumble the tofu into the pan. Sprinkle the turmeric on top and stir until the tofu is coated in the spice.

5   Add the soy sauce, mushrooms and parsley. Continue cooking for 6 minutes, or until most of the moisture has evaporated.

6   Take the pan off the heat and stir in the nutritional yeast. Season with salt and ground black pepper, to taste.

7   This scramble is delicious served on slices of warm whole grain toast. Any leftovers can be stored in an airtight container in the refrigerator for five days. They make a great filling for lunchbox pittas.

Seven Super Sandwiches

As you'll see in this book, there are very few foods that I won't consider stuffing into a sandwich. Any veggies left over from curries, stir fries and roasts are perfect for filling next day's pitta breads or tortilla wraps and packing into lunchboxes. However, I also love experimenting with new filling combinations and the more colourful the better! Over the next couple of pages you'll find a selection of our family favourites. All of them come together in a matter of minutes, making them perfect when you need to grab a quick bite at lunchtime or prepare for a 'lunch on the go'.

1. Falafel, Hummus, Beetroot Salad & Sweet Pickle

At home, we serve this filling with lightly toasted granary bread or wrapped in flour tortillas. For lunchboxes, we stuff it into wholemeal pitta breads so, no matter how much the school bag gets shaken, the filling stays neatly inside. For this sandwich, we either use home-made falafel (p79) or store-bought.

2. Cheese, Tomato & Basil

This is a pretty classic combination, except that we use vegan 'cheese'. In our dairy-eating days, none of us actually liked cheese slices, but we really like the Violife slices (available in the UK from major supermarkets and health food stores). They're made with coconut oil instead of cow's milk and are surprisingly tasty.

3. Sweet Chilli Chickpea Smash

Chickpea smashes are really versatile. You can flavour them in different ways and change the texture, making them coarse or creamy. One of our all-time favourites is made with a can of drained chickpeas, glug of sweet chilli sauce, splash of fresh lime juice and pinch of salt whizzed in a food processor until coarse. Serve in a sandwich with organic sprouts or salad leaves and a generous sprinkling of freshly ground black pepper.

4. Mediterranean Veggie Ciabatta

This is one of our favourite Saturday night teas. A selection of colourful veggies (red onion, courgette, bell pepper, mushrooms) and seeds (sunflower & pumpkin) are pan-fried, then served on crispy, warm ciabatta slathered in sun-dried tomato paste or pesto (p103). The veggies are either fried in a drizzle of olive oil with plenty of seasoning or a splash of tamari soy sauce.

5. Chocolate Hazelnut Spread & Banana Panini

This sandwich is perfect for 'elevenses', or for whenever a sweet craving strikes. Slice the panini in half and toast it. Cover one side of the panini in chocolate hazelnut spread (I make a quick home-made spread by whizzing together hazelnut butter, maple syrup, cocoa powder, a little coconut oil and pinch of salt in my food processor). Spread mashed ripe banana on the other side and sprinkle on some cinnamon. Slam the two sides together and devour.

6. Smoked Tofu, Avocado & Tomato Salad

I was so pleased to find smoked tofu in the Spanish supermarket Hipercor so we could make one of our favourite sandwiches whilst on vacation – smoked tofu, sliced tomato and avocado, beetroot salad and hummus, topped with a sprinkling of salt and freshly ground black pepper. For our return flight, we stuffed this filling into seeded whole wheat mini baguettes. It tasted so good and far better than any food available on the plane. Back home, we use the Taifun organic smoked tofu, currently available in the UK from Waitrose, Ocado and health food shops.

7. The Sunday Dinner Super Sandwich

We used to call this the 'Boxing Day Sandwich' as it was filled with our Christmas Dinner leftovers. However, I love this sandwich so much that I couldn't relegate it to a 'once a year' thing. Now we use the leftovers from the Sunday roast dinner, or I even just make this sandwich instead of a Sunday roast, hence why Lil' L calls it the 'Sunday Dinner sandwich'. The components of this sandwich are Cranberry-Glazed Nut Loaf (p140) and Brussels Sprout Hash (p76), served on soft granary bread with a drizzle of cranberry sauce.

Chive & Onion Frittata
with Sun-Dried Tomato

Serves: 3-4   Hands on: 20 minutes   Ready in: 35 minutes

In contrast to egg omelettes and frittatas which I couldn't stand as a child (I can't bear the eggy flavour), I absolutely adore their plant-based counterpart. They're a huge hit with the rest of the family too. This frittata makes a great lunch or light dinner option. We love to serve it with mixed baby salad leaves and a dollop of hummus or vegan mayonnaise.

2 TBSP olive oil, divided

2 medium onions (250g), finely diced

1-2 garlic cloves, minced

60ml / ¼ cup soya milk

300g / 10½ oz silken tofu, drained

1-2 tsp Dijon mustard

1 TBSP tahini

45g / ⅓ cup gram flour (aka besan flour, chickpea flour, garbanzo bean flour)

2 TBSP nutritional yeast flakes

2 TBSP cornflour (cornstarch)

¼ tsp ground turmeric

½ tsp salt (use black salt if you want an 'eggy' flavour)

6-8 sun-dried tomatoes in olive oil, drained and diced

1 small bunch of chives (25g), chopped

1   Gently heat ½ TBSP oil in a non-stick ovenproof frying pan (skillet). Add the onions and cook for 4 minutes on medium heat. Add the garlic and cook for a further minute, then remove from the heat.

2   Place the milk, tofu, mustard, tahini and 1 TBSP olive oil in a mixing bowl and blend smooth using a hand blender (alternatively use a jug blender). Add the gram flour, nutritional yeast, cornflour, turmeric and salt, and blend to combine. Fold in the cooked onions and garlic, sun-dried tomatoes and most of the chives (reserve a small handful for the garnish).

3   Coat the bottom of the frying pan with ½ TBSP oil and pour in the frittata mixture. Use a spatula to distribute the mixture evenly in the pan. Sprinkle the reserved chives on top and lightly press down. Cook for 15 minutes on medium-low heat, or until the edges start to firm up.

4   Towards the end of the cooking time, preheat the grill (broiler). Place the frying pan under the grill (with the handle sticking out) until the frittata is lightly browned (about 3 minutes). Keep a watch on it as it can burn quickly. Using an oven glove, remove the pan from the oven. Leave to rest for at least 5 minutes (it will firm up as it cools), then loosen with a slotted turner and slide onto a chopping board. Slice into segments and serve.

5   The frittata can be stored in the refrigerator for three days. It can be eaten cold or gently warmed through before serving.

TIP   An easy way to chop chives is to snip them using kitchen scissors.

THE GOOD STUFF ♥

Onions are great immune-boosters and are packed with antibacterial, anti-inflammatory and antiviral nutrients. Red onions are an especially rich source of antioxidant flavonoids, which have a host of health benefits, including promotion of a strong immune system and cardiovascular health.

Green Pea Tostadas
with Avocado & Sun-Dried Tomato

Serves: 4   Hands on: 20 minutes   Ready in: 20 minutes

These tostadas are one of my favourite spring/summer meals. The green peas add pops of sweetness which pairs really well with the sun-dried tomatoes and the buttery avocado. These tostadas are filling enough to serve as a main meal, especially when accompanied with a side salad. They're easy to prepare, making them perfect for busy weekdays or whenever you need a quick meal.

4 large seeded or whole grain soft tortillas (use GF tortillas, if needed)

260g / 2 cups frozen green peas

8-10 sun-dried tomatoes in olive oil, drained and diced

2 ripe avocados

200g / ¾ cup hummus

2 TBSP shelled hemp seeds

freshly ground black pepper (omit for children)

1   Preheat the oven to 200C (180C fan) / 200F. Place the tortillas on baking trays and bake for 7 minutes, or until they are starting to brown all over. (Depending on the size of the tortillas you may need to bake in two batches). Remove from the oven and immediately slice into quarters. As they cool, they will crisp up.

2   While the tortillas are baking, prepare the toppings. Place the frozen green peas in a frying pan (skillet) and cook on medium heat until they are thawed through and vibrant green in colour. Scoop out the avocado flesh and finely dice.

3   When the tortillas are baked, spread some hummus onto each quarter. Arrange the sun-dried tomato and avocado pieces on top, followed by a sprinkling of green peas. Press down lightly so the toppings stick to the hummus.

4   Sprinkle on some shelled hemp seeds and ground black pepper (if desired), and serve immediately.

THE GOOD STUFF ♥

Avocados are a rich source of monounsaturated fats, which are anti-inflammatory, help to lower cholesterol levels and promote heart health. They also contain protein, carbohydrate, vitamins, minerals and a range of powerful antioxidants, including betacarotene, alphacarotene, lutein and vitamin E.

Brussels Sprout Hash
with Balsamic Red Onion & Pecans

Serves: 3-4   Hands on: 20 minutes   Ready in: 20 minutes

If you know anyone that proclaims to hate sprouts, encourage them to give this recipe a try. Sliced and fried, Brussels sprouts take on a nutty flavour and crisp texture that's far removed from their boiled and steamed counterparts. This is the recipe that transformed Lil' L from a sprout hater to sprout lover. When he was small, he would leave any sprouts that I optimistically placed on his plate. After one taste of this Hash though, he declared it to be delicious and wolfed it down. To this day, it remains one of my family's favourite dishes. As a light meal option, we like to serve it with brown rice pan-fried in olive oil and soy sauce, or stuffed into our Sunday Dinner sandwich (p71). It's also perfect for serving as a side dish for roast dinners (p140).

60g / ½ cup pecans

1 TBSP olive oil, divided

1 medium red onion (130g), thinly sliced

½ TBSP coconut sugar or unrefined cane sugar

1 TBSP balsamic vinegar

500g / about 20-25 medium Brussels sprouts, fresh or defrosted, trimmed and thinly sliced

½ tsp salt

freshly ground black pepper, to taste (omit if serving to small children)

1   In a small frying pan (skillet), toast the pecans on medium-high heat, stirring continuously. When they start to become fragrant, test one. If they have an intense nutty flavour, they are done. Tip them onto a plate and set to one side.

2   Turn down the heat to medium-low, add ½ TBSP oil to the pan and cook the onion for about 8 minutes, stirring now and then. Stir in the sugar and vinegar and continue cooking until most of the vinegar has evaporated, then remove from the heat.

3   While the onion is cooking, prepare the Brussels sprouts. In a large frying pan (skillet) heat the remaining oil on medium-high. Add the sprouts and season with salt and ground black pepper. Stir fry until they are browned (about 6 minutes).

4   When ready, add the onion and pecans to the sprouts and stir through to combine. Taste test and add more seasoning if required.

5   This dish is delicious served warm or cold. Any leftovers can be stored in the refrigerator for five days.

THE GOOD STUFF ♥

Brussels sprouts have powerful detoxifying and anti-inflammatory properties. They contain more than 20 essential vitamins and minerals, and are a rich source of antioxidant phytonutrients including glucosinolates, which boost the immune system and help protect against disease. Just one cup of cooked sprouts provides 274% of the vitamin K RDA and 162% of vitamin C.

THE GOOD STUFF ♥
Chickpeas (aka garbanzo beans) are a great source of
protein, dietary fibre, B vitamins and minerals. Just one cup
of cooked chickpeas provides 84% of the manganese RDA
and 26% of iron. Chickpeas also contain an abundance of
phytonutrients, including flavonoids and phenolic acids, which
have a powerful antioxidant effect on the body.

Moroccan-Spiced Falafel

Serves: 4-5   Hands on: 30 minutes   Ready in: 60 minutes

Falafel originated in the Middle East but is now a popular street food all over the world. By making them yourself, you can adjust the flavours, leaving them mild for children, or spicing them up for the heat lovers in the family. Though not traditional, we love our falafel flavoured with the warming sweet and savoury spices of Morocco. Our favourite way to serve them is stuffed into pitta breads or tortilla wraps along with hummus, salad, avocado, sweet pickle and a sprinkling of hemp seeds.

1 TBSP olive oil, divided

1 red onion (130g), finely diced

2-3 garlic cloves, minced

1 red bell pepper, deseeded and finely diced

1 tsp ground cumin

1 tsp sweet paprika

½ tsp ground cinnamon

¼ tsp ground ginger

400g / 14 oz can chickpeas, rinsed and thoroughly drained

small handful of fresh parsley or coriander leaves (cilantro), chopped

2 TBSP chopped pitted dates

2 TBSP chopped dried apricots

2 TBSP sesame seeds

½ tsp bicarbonate of soda (baking soda)

½ tsp salt

90g / 1 cup rolled oats (quick oats, not jumbo)

2 TBSP flour (any kind), for coating

1   Gently heat ½ TBSP oil in a large non-stick frying pan (skillet) and cook the onion, garlic and bell pepper for 2 minutes. Stir in the dry spices, then remove from the heat.

2   Place the chickpeas in a fine mesh sieve. Rinse under cold water then shake vigorously to remove all the water droplets.

3   Place the contents of the frying pan, the chickpeas, parsley/coriander, dates, apricots, sesame seeds, bicarbonate of soda, salt and oats in a food processor and blend to make a coarse paste. Place in the refrigerator for at least 30 minutes to allow the mixture to firm up (it can be left overnight).

4   Tip the flour onto a plate. Scoop a heaped tablespoon of the falafel mixture. Roll lightly in the flour, shake off any excess flour, then flatten the falafel slightly. Repeat until all the mixture is used up.

5   If possible, use two frying pans (skillets) to halve the cooking time. Coat the bottom of the pan with oil. Cook the falafel on medium heat until browned on the underside (about 4 minutes). Flip them over and cook for a further 3 minutes or so. Leave to cool for a couple of minutes before serving (the falafel will firm up as they cool).

6   These falafel are delicious served warm or cold. They will keep for three days in the refrigerator. They also freeze well.

Sun-Dried Tomato Hummus

Yield: about 330g / 11/2 cups   Hands on: 5 minutes   Ready in: 5 minutes

Hummus ('houmous') is so versatile! It makes a tasty snack or starter served with vegetable crudités, dip for tortilla chips, filling for sandwiches and wraps, and accompaniment to salads. We love experimenting with different flavour combinations, and one of our all-time favourites is sun-dried tomato with Dukkah spice. In contrast to traditional hummus recipes, I prefer to blend the chickpeas with water rather than oil. I find that it doesn't compromise the flavour, yet it greatly reduces the calorie content, which is a bonus for 'hummus monsters' like me!

400g / 14 oz can chickpeas, drained and liquid reserved
1 TBSP tahini
1½ TBSP sun-dried tomato paste
1 TBSP freshly squeezed lemon or lime juice
1 tsp ground cumin

½ tsp salt
1 garlic clove, minced (either raw or lightly fried in olive oil), optional

Garnish
Dukkah spice mix (we love Olives et al)

1   Place all the ingredients in a food processor (or use a bowl and hand blender). Add 4 TBSP of the reserved chickpea water and blend smooth. Add a splash more liquid, if needed. Taste test and adjust the seasoning, if desired.

2   Spoon into a bowl, sprinkle on the garnish and serve. This hummus will keep for three days in the refrigerator. It also freezes well.

TIP   To make Classic Hummus, simply omit the sun-dried tomato paste.

Quick Vegetable Couscous

Serves: 4   Hands on: 10 minutes   Ready in: 10 minutes

Couscous is perfect for serving with Moroccan dishes. I find it also goes well with curry dishes and makes a quick and easy substitute for rice. As a rule of thumb, I use a ratio of ⅓ cup of couscous to ½ cup of liquid per serving.

We serve the recipe below as an accompaniment to Nut Koftas (p82) and Falafel (p79). To transform the dish itself into a main meal, add a drained can of kidney beans and serve with a generous dollop of hummus and colourful salad leaves.

250g / 1⅓ cups whole wheat couscous
480ml / 2 cups vegetable stock (broth)
1 TBSP olive oil, divided

1 small red onion (90g), diced
1 small red bell pepper (140g), deseeded and diced
90g / ½ cup frozen green peas
½ - 1 tsp each of dried oregano, smoked paprika and ground cumin

1   Prepare a jug of boiling hot vegetable stock. Place the couscous in a heat-proof dish. Pour the stock on top, stir through and cover with a lid or plate for 7 minutes. Drizzle in ½ TBSP oil and fluff up the grains with a fork.

2   Meanwhile heat ½ TBSP oil in a large frying pan (skillet) on medium heat. Add the vegetables and spices, and cook for 4-5 minutes, stirring regularly. When the couscous is ready, combine with the pan-fried veggies. Taste test and adjust the seasoning to suit.

3   This dish can be served hot and cold. It will keep for three days in the refrigerator. It also freezes well.

THE GOOD STUFF ♥
Dried herbs and spices aren't just great for flavouring food - they also add a powerful dose of antioxidants, so be sure to sprinkle liberally!

Nut Koftas

Serves: 4   Hands on: 30 minutes   Ready in: 30 minutes

Koftas are a Middle Eastern food, traditionally made of ground beef or lamb. In our version, the animals have been replaced with heart-healthy, nutrient-rich nuts. For a main meal, we love to serve the koftas on a bed of Quick Vegetable Couscous (p81) with a generous dollop of Hummus (p80). They also make a great lunchbox option, stuffed into pitta breads or wrapped in a flat bread, with salad and pickle.

1½ TBSP olive oil, divided

1 medium onion (130g), finely diced

2-3 garlic cloves, minced

1 tsp curry powder (use mild for children)

1 TBSP natural peanut butter

400g / 14 oz can black eye beans (aka black eyed peas), thoroughly drained

75g / ½ cup mixed nuts (I use cashews and walnuts)

100g / 1 cup ground almonds (almond meal)

50g / ½ cup rolled oats (quick oats, not jumbo)

¼ tsp salt

1   Heat ½ TBSP oil in a large frying pan (skillet) and sauté the onion for a couple of minutes. Add the garlic and curry powder and cook for a further minute. Stir in the peanut butter, then remove from the heat.

2   Place the black eye beans in a fine mesh sieve. Rinse under cold water, then shake vigorously to remove all the water droplets.

3   Pulse the mixed nuts in a food processor to break them up. Add the beans, ground almonds, onion mixture, oats and salt, and process until the mixture is fully combined. Taste test and adjust the seasoning, if desired.

4   Place the mixture in the refrigerator for 30 minutes (can be left overnight).

5   Roll the mixture into sixteen ping pong size balls. Gently push the balls onto four metal skewers (about 20cm / 8 inches in length).

6   Coat the bottom of the frying pan with the remaining oil. Add the koftas and cook for about 10 minutes on medium heat, turning regularly so that they brown evenly all over. Leave to rest for a couple of minutes before serving (they will firm up as they cool).

7   These koftas are delicious served hot or cold. They will keep for three days in the refrigerator or weeks in the freezer.

THE GOOD STUFF ♥

Almonds are one of the richest sources of the antioxidant vitamin E, which helps to promote healthy skin. They are also a great source of protein, dietary fibre, heart-healthy monounsaturated fats and minerals. One cup of ground almonds provides 125% of the vitamin E RDA, 25% of calcium and 20% of iron.

Moroccan Fruity Couscous

Serves: 4   Hands on: 20 minutes   Ready in: 20 minutes

This gently spiced, fruity couscous makes a lovely summer weekend lunch or speedy weekday supper. It's equally delicious served hot or cold, making it perfect for al fresco dining and picnics. As a main meal, we like to serve it with strips of warm pitta bread, hummus and baby salad leaves. I've kept it mild enough for children, but feel free to spice it up with some chilli or cayenne pepper.

245g / 1⅓ cups whole wheat couscous

6-8 sun-dried tomatoes in olive oil, drained and diced

8 dried apricots, diced

30g / 3 TBSP dried cranberries or sultanas

480ml / 2 cups boiling hot vegetable stock (broth)

1 TBSP olive oil, divided

1 medium onion (140g), diced

2-3 garlic cloves, minced

1 bell pepper (190g), deseeded and diced (or use a mix of different coloured pepper pieces to make it extra vibrant)

1 medium courgette (zucchini) (240g), quartered lengthwise and sliced

1 tsp ground cumin

½ - 1 tsp sweet paprika

½ tsp ground cinnamon

¼ tsp ground ginger

¼ tsp ground turmeric

small handful of fresh coriander leaves (cilantro) or parsley, roughly chopped

salt, to taste

4 TBSP toasted flaked almonds

2 TBSP toasted sesame seeds

1   Place the couscous, sun-dried tomatoes, dried apricots and cranberries/sultanas in a heat-proof bowl. Pour the boiling hot stock on top, cover with a lid or plate and leave for 7 minutes. Drizzle on ½ TBSP olive oil and fluff up with a fork.

2   Meanwhile, heat ½ TBSP oil in a large frying pan (skillet) on medium heat and cook the onion, garlic, bell pepper and courgette for a couple of minutes. Stir in the dried spices, reduce the heat to medium-low and continue cooking for 5 minutes. If the vegetables start to stick, add a splash of water to the pan.

3   Once ready, tip the couscous into the pan along with the fresh herbs. Gently stir through to combine. Season with salt to taste.

4   Divide between four bowls. Sprinkle on the nuts and seeds, and serve.

5   Any leftovers can be stored in the refrigerator for three days. They're great for packing into lunchboxes as an alternative to sandwiches. This dish also freezes well.

SUPER SPEEDY VERSION

To save on chopping time, substitute the fresh vegetables with a bag of frozen grilled Mediterranean vegetables.

THE GOOD STUFF ♥

Apricots are rich in carotenoids including the
powerful antioxidant lycopene. They are also a good
source of dietary fibre, vitamin A, vitamin E, and
minerals, including potassium, copper and iron.

Baked Onion Bhajis

Serves: 3-4   Hands on: 20 minutes   Ready in: 45 minutes

You may never have considered onion bhajis to be a healthy meal option, but I promise they can be! While bhajis are traditionally deep fried, I simply bake them in the oven. They're sweet, tender and exceedingly tasty! We love to serve the bhajis wrapped in giant flat breads (like flour tortillas) with shredded lettuce, red cabbage and carrot, drizzled in mango chutney (recipe overleaf) or sweet pickle. They're also delicious stuffed into pittas to make 'Bhaji Kebabs'. They make a very tasty addition to school and work lunchboxes!

1 TBSP olive oil

4 medium onions (520g), sliced into thin strips about 2.5cm / 1 inch long

2 garlic cloves, minced

1 TBSP tomato purée (paste)

1-2 tsp curry powder (use mild for children)

2 TBSP coriander leaves (cilantro), finely chopped

55g / 6 TBSP gram flour (aka besan flour, chickpea flour, garbanzo bean flour)

¼ tsp salt

1 TBSP water

1   Preheat the oven to 180C (160C fan) / 350F. Line a large baking sheet with non-stick baking paper.

2   Add 1 TBSP oil to a large non-stick frying pan (skillet) and cook the onions on medium heat for 4 minutes.

3   Add the garlic and cook for a further minute.

4   Stir in the tomato purée, curry powder and coriander leaves, then remove from the heat.

5   Sprinkle in the gram flour and salt. Add a tablespoon of water and stir until fully combined. The mixture should start to stick together. If it is too dry add a splash more water.

6   Scoop up a heaping tablespoon of the mixture and place on the baking sheet. Repeat to make seven more bhajis. With damp hands, lightly press down to flatten the tops.

7   Bake for 20 minutes, or until the bhajis are dry to the touch. Leave to rest for a couple of minutes (they will firm up as they cool), then use a thin spatula to remove them from the baking paper.

8   Stored in an airtight container, the bhajis will keep for up to a week in the refrigerator. They also freeze well. Bake straight from frozen for about 9 minutes.

Mango Chutney

Yield: about 210g / 1 cup   Hands on: 5 minutes   Ready in: 15 minutes

This mango chutney is a delicious accompaniment for Onion Bhajis (p86) and Indian-spiced burgers (p125). It tastes so fresh and is far less sugary than the store-bought chutneys. It's super easy to make too.

1 medium mango (390g), flesh diced or
215g / 1⅓ cups frozen mango chunks

5g root ginger (½ inch piece), finely grated

30ml / 2 TBSP apple cider vinegar

25g / 2 TBSP unrefined cane sugar

pinch of salt

1   Place all the ingredients in a small saucepan. Bring to the boil, then reduce the heat and simmer for about 5 minutes. As the mango starts to soften, mash it with a wooden spoon to break it down. Allow to cool slightly, then taste test and add more sweetener, if desired.

2   For a smooth chutney, blend to a smooth consistency using a hand or jug blender.

3   This chutney will keep for five days in the refrigerator. It also freezes well.

Chickpea Pancakes

Serves: 3-4   Hands on: 20 minutes   Ready in: 20 minutes

These pancakes are made with gram flour (ground chickpeas), which is a nutrient-rich, high protein, gluten-free flour. They are quick, easy to make and versatile. We often fill them with leftover Thai or Indian curry, Italian Bolognese or Mexican Chilli. For a speedy lunch, we love chopped avocado drizzled with sweet chilli sauce, or veggies sautéed in soy sauce. I also like to add some finely chopped red chilli and coriander leaves to the batter for extra flavour and colour.

120g / 1 cup gram flour (aka besan flour, chickpea flour, garbanzo bean flour)

70g / ½ cup fine wholemeal (whole wheat pastry) flour, chapatti flour or GF flour mix

350ml / 1½ cups unsweetened soya milk

1 TBSP olive oil

1 tsp baking powder

½ tsp salt

seasoning of choice (I often use 1 tsp each of dried oregano and sweet paprika)

½ TBSP organic rapeseed (canola) oil or other neutral-flavoured oil, for frying

Optional extras

1 red chilli, deseeded and finely chopped

2 TBSP fresh coriander leaves (cilantro), finely chopped

1   Place all the ingredients in a tall jug and whiz with a hand blender until smooth. Leave the batter to rest for a few minutes (this can happen while the pan warms up). Whisk in any of the optional extras.

2   If possible, use two non-stick frying pans (skillets) to halve the cooking time. Brush the bottom of the pan with oil and preheat on medium heat. Flick a drop of water in the pan and if it sizzles the pan is ready.

3   Pour ⅓ cup of batter into the pan and swirl to thin out. When the pancake starts to firm up, flip it over using a slotted turner and continue cooking for 30 seconds or so. Repeat with the remaining batter, brushing the pan with oil each time. Keep the pancakes in a warm oven until ready to serve.

4   These pancakes will keep for three days in the refrigerator. Gently warm through before serving. Stored pancakes will become less flexible over time and can break when folded, so place the veggies on top rather than filling and folding.

SOME OF OUR FAVOURITE FILLINGS:
♥ Thai Curry (p110)
♥ Indian-Spiced Sweet Potato Curry (p120)
♥ Veggie 'Bolognese' (p100)
♥ Mushrooms, bell pepper and courgette (zucchini) sautéed in soy sauce
♥ Chopped avocado, toasted sunflower seeds, shelled hemp seeds and sweet chilli sauce

Sun-Dried Tomato Quiche
with Roasted Tenderstem & Red Pepper

Serves: 6   Hands on: 30 minutes   Ready in: 90 minutes

This quiche is perfect for serving at lunch parties, buffets and picnics. The filling is packed full of flavour and encased in a pastry which is robust enough to be sliced and handled without crumbling. If you wish, you could always cheat and buy ready-made pastry but I promise you, the recipe overleaf is incredibly easy to make (and cheap too!) The quiche can be eaten hot or cold. As a main meal, we like to serve it with a big green salad and a side helping of baked beans.

Pastry crust

140g / 1 cup wholemeal (whole wheat pastry) flour or chapatti flour

140g / 1 cup plain (all purpose) flour

¼ tsp salt

100g / ½ cup dairy-free spread/vegan butter or aroma-free coconut butter

5-8 TBSP water

Filling

120g / 1 handful of tenderstem broccoli, stalks diced

1 sweet romano or red bell pepper (190g), deseeded and sliced

1 garlic clove, minced

1 large onion (170g), sliced into thin wedges

1 TBSP & 1 tsp olive oil

400g / 14 oz firm tofu

½ tsp salt

1 tsp Dijon mustard

2 TBSP nutritional yeast flakes

1 tsp dried dill or oregano

small handful of fresh basil leaves, shredded

6-8 sun-dried tomatoes in olive oil, drained and diced

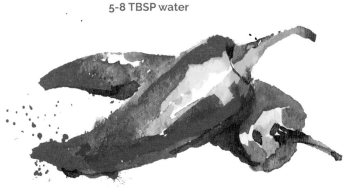

1   Preheat the oven to 200C (180C fan) / 400F. Grease a 23cm / 9 inch loose-bottomed quiche tin.

2   Place the flours, salt and dairy-free spread/butter in a food processor and whiz to combine. Add water through the funnel, a little at a time, until the mixture starts to come together. The amount needed will vary depending on the type of flour and butter used.

3   Press the pastry into the quiche tin. Be sure to press it right into the edges of the tin and all the way up the sides. Prick the pastry all over with a fork.

4   Place the broccoli, red pepper, garlic and onion in a large roasting tin. Drizzle in 1 TBSP olive oil and stir through.

5   Place both the pastry and veggies in the oven and bake for 20 minutes, or until cooked through. I find the pastry doesn't colour, but it should be dry to the touch. The veggies should just be starting to brown.

6   Drain the tofu and squeeze to remove as much water as possible. Crumble the tofu into a food processor. Add 1 tsp olive oil, salt, mustard and nutritional yeast, and whiz smooth. Add the roasted onion, dried dill/oregano and basil leaves, and pulse to combine. Tip the mixture into a large bowl.

7   Reserve some roasted broccoli, red pepper and sun-dried tomato pieces for decorating the top, then add the remaining veggies to the tofu mixture and stir to combine. Tip the mixture onto the pastry crust and press down to smooth and level. Press the reserved veggies into the top.

8   Bake at 180C (160C fan) / 350F for 35 minutes, or until the tofu is lightly golden on top. Leave the quiche to cool slightly before slicing (it will firm up as it cools). The quiche will keep for five days stored in an airtight container in the refrigerator.

Veggie Pasties

Serves: 6   Hands on: 30 minutes   Ready in: 1 hour 40 minutes

'Pastie' is another word that we don't normally associate with 'healthy', but these home-made pasties are packed with goodness. The pastry's made with wholemeal flour and we've crammed as many veggies inside as we could possibly fit. While they are most delicious served freshly baked, they can also be eaten cold and make a tasty treat for lunchboxes and picnics.

Pastry

140g / 1 cup fine wholemeal (whole wheat pastry) flour or chapatti flour

140g / 1 cup plain (all purpose) flour or chapatti flour

¼ tsp salt

100g / ½ cup dairy-free spread/vegan butter or aroma-free coconut butter

5-8 TBSP cold water

soya milk, for glaze

Filling

3 packed cups' worth of mixed vegetables (about 450g / 16 oz), finely diced (e.g. 1 small onion, 1 small sweet potato, 1 small carrot, 1 small red bell pepper, 2 white cabbage leaves, 1 large handful of spinach)

2 TBSP parsley, finely chopped

1 tsp each dried thyme, dried oregano

1 tsp vegetable bouillon powder

1 tsp Dijon mustard

¼ tsp salt

1   Place the flours, salt and dairy-free spread/butter in a food processor and whiz to combine. Add water through the funnel, a little at a time, until the crumbs start to come together. The amount of water needed will vary depending on the type of flour and butter used. Scoop the dough into a ball, wrap in cling film (plastic wrap) and chill for 30 minutes.

2   Preheat the oven to 190C (170C fan) / 375F. Line a large baking sheet with non-stick baking paper.

3   Mix all the filling ingredients together in a large bowl. If using spinach, first wilt it by placing it in a strainer and pouring boiling water on top. Run under cold water to cool it down, squeeze hard to remove the excess water then roughly chop.

4   Divide the pastry into six balls (I weigh my pastry to divide it equally). On a lightly floured surface, roll each ball into a circle with an 18cm / 7 inch diameter (I use a side plate as a template). Place ½ cup of vegetables on one half of the circle, leaving a small border. Brush the pastry edge with a little milk or water. Fold the pastry over to form a half moon. Crimp the edge using a fork or knife handle, to seal. Repeat for the remaining five pasties.

5   Place the pasties on the prepared baking sheet. Brush the tops with milk and pierce twice to allow the steam to escape. Bake for 40 minutes, or until the pasties are dry to the touch.

6   Stored in an airtight container, these pasties will keep in the refrigerator for five days. They can also be frozen prior to baking.

THE GOOD STUFF ♥
Parsley is far more worthy of 'superfood' status
than its typical relegation as a garnish. It is a nutritional
powerhouse, packed full of antioxidant phytonutrients
including flavonoids and vitamins A, C and K. Just one
tablespoon of parsley contains 77% of the recommended
daily amount of anti-inflammatory vitamin K.

Avocado & Black Bean Nachos

Serves: 4   Hands on: 20 minutes   Ready in: 35 minutes

This is one of our favourite Saturday 'movie night' dinners. It's simple to prepare and all the components can easily be made in advance. Nachos are often served slathered in melted cheese but, in our version, we use a delicious dairy-free 'cheesy' sauce that is packed full of goodness (we've even managed to sneak some veggies in there!)

Smoky 'Queso' Sauce (p95)

Sweet Chilli Salsa (p95) or your favourite shop-bought salsa

2 ripe avocados, diced

squeeze of fresh lime juice, optional

salt and ground black pepper, to taste

400g / 14 oz can black beans, rinsed and drained

250g / 9 oz tortilla chips

2 TBSP fresh coriander leaves (cilantro), chopped, for garnish

1   First, prepare the Smoky 'Queso' Sauce using the recipe overleaf. While the veggies are roasting, prepare the Sweet Chilli Salsa and chop the avocados. If not serving immediately, toss the chopped avocados in lime juice to prevent them from blackening. Season with salt and pepper, to taste.

2   Arrange the tortilla chips on heat-proof plates. Place most of the chips around the outer edge so that they stay crisp and easy to pick up without getting messy fingers. Sprinkle on the salsa, avocados, black beans and Smoky 'Queso' Sauce. Place in a preheated oven at 200C (180C fan) / 400F for 5 minutes, or until warmed through. Be careful when removing from the oven as the plates will be very hot! Garnish with chopped coriander leaves and serve.

Sweet Chilli Salsa

Serves: 4   Hands on: 5 minutes   Ready in: 15 minutes

Traditional salsa recipes include jalapeno, raw onion and coriander which can be overpowering, especially for children. We prefer to omit them and let the fresh tomato flavour shine through.

4 large ripe organic tomatoes (450g), diced
1 TBSP extra virgin olive oil
1 TBSP fresh lime juice
1 tsp sweet chilli sauce, or to taste (omit if serving to small children)

1 tsp unrefined sugar
1 tsp dried oregano
½ tsp ground cumin
¼ tsp salt

1   Place all the ingredients in a bowl and stir through to combine. Taste test and adjust the seasoning to suit. Leave for a few minutes for the flavours to meld before serving. The salsa will keep for up to five days in the refrigerator.

Smoky 'Queso' Sauce

Serves: 4-6   Hands on: 10 minutes   Ready in: 25 minutes

This Mexican-inspired sauce has a delicious smoky flavour with a hint of cheesiness, thanks to the nutritional yeast. It makes a great cheese substitute for nachos, and can also be used as a jacket potato topping, pasta sauce or dip for vegetable crudités.

1 orange, yellow or red bell pepper (180g), deseeded and sliced
1 medium onion (140g), sliced into thin wedges
2 garlic cloves, minced
1 tsp smoked paprika

1 TBSP olive oil
180ml / ¾ cup unsweetened soya milk
100g / ¾ cup raw cashews
1 TBSP fresh lime juice
14g / 4 TBSP nutritional yeast flakes
½ tsp salt

1   Preheat the oven to 200C (180C fan) / 400F. Place the bell pepper, onion and garlic in a roasting tin. Sprinkle on the paprika. Drizzle on the oil and stir through. Roast for 15 minutes, stirring halfway through.

2   If you don't have a high powered blender, boil the cashews in a pan of water for 15 minutes to soften them, then rinse and drain.

3   Add all the ingredients to a blender and blend on high speed until silky smooth, stopping now and then to scrape down the sides. Taste test and adjust the seasoning to suit.

4   This dip will keep for five days in the refrigerator. It also freezes really well. It may thicken over time, so whisk in a splash more milk to reach the desired consistency.

Mains

For this chapter, I've chosen a selection of our all-time favourite evening meals. Most of them require 30 minutes or less hands-on time, but some benefit from being prepared an hour or so in advance. By checking the 'Ready in' time, you'll see which dishes are worth preparing as soon as you get home from work or school, or those best saved for a weekend.

While I provide a list of vegetables for each dish, feel free to substitute with your favourite veggies. Most of the recipes are very flexible, so you can easily adapt them to suit your own tastes. My choice of vegetables is often down to what I find in the refrigerator and what needs using up!

All these dishes are designed to be suitable for the whole family, and I've been serving them to Lil' L since he was a pre-schooler. In the early years, I finely chopped or roughly blended his portion using my hand blender, then gradually increased the size of the veggies. Since nuts and seeds can be a choking hazard for small children, always make sure they're chopped or whiz them in a food processor before adding them to their dish.

THE GOOD STUFF ♥
In natural medicine, mushrooms are revered for their healing qualities and their ability to stimulate the immune system to ward off disease. They are especially rich in antioxidant phytonutrients, B vitamins, copper and selenium.

Quick Sun-Dried Tomato Fusilli
with Green Beans & Mushrooms

Serves: 4   Hands on: 15 minutes   Ready in: 15 minutes

This pasta dish is perfect for busy weekdays. It's simple and quick to prepare, and can be served hot or cold. Any leftovers can be packed into lunchboxes for school and work.

300g / 10½ oz whole wheat Fusilli (use GF pasta, if needed)

125g / 1¼ cups fresh or frozen fine green beans, trimmed and halved

2 TBSP pine nuts

1 medium red onion (130g), diced

2 garlic cloves, minced

150g / 2 cups chestnut (or crimini) mushrooms, chopped

2 TBSP mixed seeds (e.g. sunflower and pumpkin)

3 TBSP sun-dried tomato paste

8 sun-dried tomatoes in olive oil, drained and diced (reserve the oil)

16-20 pitted black olives

nutritional yeast flakes or Cashew 'Parmesan' (p101), for sprinkling

1   Prepare a large pan of boiling water. Add the pasta. 5 minutes into the cooking time, add the green beans. Bring back to the boil and continue cooking for 7 minutes, or until the pasta is al dente. Drain, then return the pasta and beans to the pan and stir in the sun-dried tomato paste.

2   While the pasta is cooking, toast the pine nuts in a dry frying pan (skillet) on medium heat, stirring continuously. As soon as they start to brown, remove from the heat and set to one side.

3   Heat 1 TBSP oil from the sun-dried tomato jar in the frying pan and cook the onion, garlic, mushrooms and seeds on medium-low heat, stirring regularly.

4   When the pasta is ready, combine with the contents of the frying pan. Add the sun-dried tomatoes and olives, and stir through. Divide between four warm bowls. Top with the toasted pine nuts and a generous sprinkling of nutritional yeast or Cashew 'Parmesan'.

5   Any leftovers can be stored in the refrigerator for three days.

Speedy Spaghetti 'Bolognese'

Serves: 4   Hands on: 20 minutes   Ready in: 25 minutes

This is our super easy, plant-based version of the classic family favourite. We've added extra veggies to the tomato sauce to crank up the 'goodness factor' and to add more delicious flavours and textures. For kids that aren't so keen on veggies in their Bolognese, simply blend them into the tomato sauce.

1 TBSP olive oil

1 medium onion (130g), finely diced

1 celery stick (65g), finely diced

2-3 garlic cloves, minced

125g / 1½ cups mushrooms, finely diced

1 medium carrot (90g), finely grated

1 tsp dried oregano

400g / 14 oz can chopped tomatoes

400g / 14 oz can lentils, drained or 180g / 2 cups meat-free mince

2 TBSP sun-dried tomato paste

2 tsp unrefined sugar

½ tsp salt

handful of fresh basil leaves roughly chopped (reserve some for a garnish)

300g / 10½ oz whole wheat spaghetti (or GF spaghetti, if needed)

nutritional yeast flakes or Cashew 'Parmesan' (p101) for sprinkling

1   Heat the oil in a large pan and gently cook the onion and celery until they start to soften.

2   Meanwhile prepare the remaining veggies. The mushrooms can either be chopped by hand or, if you want them to disappear into the sauce, whiz them in a mini food processor.

3   Add the garlic, mushrooms, grated carrot and oregano to the pan, and stir fry on medium heat for a couple of minutes. Stir in the chopped tomatoes, lentils/meat-free mince, sun-dried tomato paste, sugar, salt and basil leaves. Bring to the boil then reduce the heat and simmer, uncovered, for 10 minutes or so. Taste test, and adjust the seasoning to suit.

4   While the Bolognese is simmering, cook the spaghetti until al dente.

5   Drain the pasta and divide between four warm bowls. Spoon the Bolognese on top and garnish with basil. Sprinkle on some nutritional yeast or Cashew 'Parmesan' and tuck in.

6   Any leftover Bolognese can be stored in the refrigerator for two days or in the freezer for weeks. (If using meat-free mince be sure to check the storage instructions on the packet).

TIP Leftover Bolognese can quickly be transformed into a Veggie Chilli with the addition of some beans and chilli sauce.

Cashew 'Parmesan'

Yield: about 85g / 1/2 cup   Hands on: 5 minutes   Ready in: 5 minutes

This dairy-free 'parmesan' uses just two nutrient-rich ingredients which are ground together to make a cheesy, savoury condiment that's perfect for sprinkling on pasta dishes.

40g / ¼ cup raw cashews
18g / ¼ cup nutritional yeast flakes

pinch of salt, optional

1   Place the ingredients in a mini food processor and pulse into fine crumbs (I use the bowl attachment that came with my hand blender). Store in an airtight jar in the refrigerator, where it will keep for weeks.

Pesto Pasta
with Roasted Vegetables

Serves: 4   Hands on: 20 minutes   Ready in: 30 minutes

Here is another quick and easy pasta dish that's perfect for weekday suppers. I love making my own pestos as they taste so fresh, but feel free to use a shop-bought jar if you prefer. In the UK, dairy-free pestos can be found on the 'Free From' aisle of supermarkets and health food stores.

2 sweet romano or small red bell peppers (300g), deseeded and sliced

1 medium red onion (130g), sliced into thin wedges

1 medium courgette (zucchini) (200g), halved lengthwise and sliced

½ medium head of broccoli (200g), cut into small florets

125g / 1½ cups chestnut (or crimini) mushrooms, chopped into chunks

2 garlic cloves, minced

2 TBSP mixed seeds (e.g. pumpkin and sunflower)

1 TBSP olive oil

salt, to taste

300g / 10½ oz whole wheat pasta (use GF pasta if needed)

4-5 TBSP pesto (p103)

nutritional yeast flakes or Cashew 'Parmesan' (p101), for sprinkling

1   Preheat the oven to 200C (180C fan) / 400F.

2   Place the vegetables and seeds in a large non-stick roasting tin. Drizzle in the oil and stir through. Season with salt. Roast for 20 minutes, or until the veggies are tender. Stir halfway through the cooking time.

3   Prepare a large pan of boiling water and cook the pasta until al dente. Drain the water and return the pasta to the pan.

4   If using home-made pesto, this can be prepared while the pasta is cooking.

5   Once the pasta is ready, stir in the pesto. Gently fold in the roasted vegetables. Serve in warm bowls with a liberal sprinkling of nutritional yeast or Cashew 'Parmesan'.

6   This pasta can be served hot or cold. It will keep for three days in the refrigerator. Any leftovers make a tasty addition to lunchboxes.

SUPER SPEEDY VERSION

To reduce the prep time, you can substitute the fresh veggies with a bag of frozen Mediterranean grilled vegetables.

Basil & Spinach Pesto

Yield: about 145g / 8 TBSP   Hands on: 5 minutes   Ready in: 5 minutes

I love experimenting with different combinations of greens, nuts and seeds to make my own pesto blends. It's amazing just how much 'good stuff' you can pack into a few tablespoons! My all-time favourite has to be this Spinach & Basil Pesto. In addition to pasta dishes, it's delicious slathered on warm toasted ciabatta or French bread, topped with pan-fried Mediterranean veggies.

20g / 1 cup fresh basil leaves

30g / 1 cup fresh spinach leaves

60g / ½ cup mixed nuts (I use raw cashews, walnuts, pine nuts)

1-2 garlic cloves, minced

2 TBSP nutritional yeast flakes

¼ tsp salt

3 TBSP extra virgin olive oil

1   If you're not a fan of raw garlic, gently fry it in a splash of olive oil until it is fragrant and lightly browned (about 1-2 minutes).

2   Add all the pesto ingredients to a food processor (or use a hand blender and bowl). Whiz until you reach the desired consistency, stopping now and then to scrape down the sides. Add a touch more oil or a splash of water, if needed, to loosen the pesto.

3   Stored in an airtight container in the refrigerator, the pesto will keep for five days. It also freezes well.

Mac 'n' Cheeze

Serves: 4   Hands on: 30 minutes   Ready in: 40 minutes

In this recipe, we've given the classic childhood favourite 'Mac 'n' Cheese' a healthy makeover. We've ditched the dairy, cholesterol and saturated fats, and replaced them with a creamy 'cheesy' sauce that's packed full of vitamins, minerals, antioxidants and heart-healthy fats. I've tasted a lot of macaroni cheeses in my time - both dairy and non-dairy - and hands down this is my favourite. Lil' L is a huge fan too (despite it featuring one of his least favourite vegetables!) If you have any self-professed cauliflower haters in the family, then encourage them to try this dish. It might just convert them.

115g / ¾ cup raw cashews

300g / 3 cups fresh or frozen small cauliflower florets

2 garlic cloves, minced

1 TBSP olive oil

240ml / 1 cup unsweetened almond or soya milk

1 TBSP fresh lemon or lime juice

40g / 2 TBSP white miso

14g / 4 TBSP nutritional yeast flakes

pinch of ground nutmeg

1 tsp onion powder (optional)

½ tsp sweet paprika (optional)

salt and ground black pepper, to taste

400g / 14 oz whole wheat macaroni or other tube pasta (use GF pasta, if needed)

Garnish

Crispy Herby Crumbs (recipe overleaf)

fresh parsley, chopped

1   Soften the cashews by either soaking in freshly boiled water for 30 minutes or boiling for 15 minutes, then rinse and drain.

2   Preheat the oven to 200C (180C fan) / 400F.

3   Place the cauliflower florets and minced garlic in a roasting tin. Drizzle in the oil and stir through. Roast for 20 minutes, or until just tender and lightly browned. Stir halfway through the cooking time.

4   Meanwhile, prepare a large pan of boiling water and cook the pasta until al dente.

5   Place the milk and cashews in a jug blender and blend smooth. Add the cooked cauliflower florets and garlic, lemon/lime juice, white miso, nutritional yeast, nutmeg and optional onion powder and sweet paprika. Blend on high speed until completely smooth. Add a splash more milk, if needed, to reach the desired consistency. Add salt and pepper, to taste.

6   Generously coat the pasta in sauce, and gently heat through. Divide between warm bowls and sprinkle on the garnish. We love to serve this dish with a bowl of baby leaf salad or Crispy Kale (p184) to share.

7   Any leftover sauce will keep for five days in the refrigerator. It also freezes really well. It thickens up over time, so whisk in a splash more milk before serving.

Herby Crispy Crumbs

Yield: about 110g / 1 1/2 cups   Hands on: 5 minutes   Ready in: 15 minutes

These crumbs smell so divine as they're baking! I always keep a jar on hand as they're great for garnishing pasta dishes. I love sprinkling them over my salad bowls too.

120g / 4 oz whole grain bread or 2 cups breadcrumbs

2 TBSP extra virgin olive oil

2 heaping TBSP Italian mixed herbs (e.g. sage, thyme, oregano, rosemary)

sea salt, optional

1 Preheat the oven to 200C (180C fan) / 200F.

2 Break the bread into pieces and whiz in a food processor into crumbs.

3 Tip the crumbs into a large roasting tin. Drizzle the oil on top and stir through. Sprinkle on the herbs, stir through again then distribute the crumbs evenly in the tin. Season with sea salt, if desired.

4 Bake for 8 minutes, or until lightly browned and crispy. Stir halfway through the cooking time. Keep an eye on them towards the end of the cooking time to make sure they don't burn.

5 Once completely cool, transfer to an airtight container and store in the refrigerator, where they will keep for weeks.

Stir Fry Noodles
in a Tangy Peanut Sauce

Serves: 4   Hands on: 20 minutes   Ready in: 20 minutes

I love the simplicity and speed of wok cooking. The veggies need only be lightly cooked, so they retain their lovely crunch and freshness. This tangy, nutty stir fry dish is one of my 'go to' dinners for busy weekdays. Using bags of ready-chopped vegetables makes the preparation a breeze.

Stir fry

1 TBSP olive oil

2 garlic cloves, minced

18g root ginger (1 inch piece), finely grated

large bag of mixed stir fry vegetables (about 600g / 21 oz)

40g / ¼ cup cashews

80g / ½ packed cup marinated or smoked tofu, cubed (p19) or substitute with another ¼ cup cashews

Peanut sauce

2 TBSP tamari or reduced-salt soy sauce

2 TBSP apple cider vinegar

1 TBSP maple syrup

3 TBSP natural peanut butter

1 TBSP water

250g / 9 oz brown rice, whole wheat or other whole grain noodles

sprinkling of toasted sesame seeds or Gomasio (p185), for garnish

1   Prepare the peanut sauce by whisking together the ingredients in a small bowl using a fork, until fully combined.

2   Heat a large pan of water for the noodles.

3   Heat the oil in a large non-stick wok or deep-sided frying pan (skillet) on medium-low heat and cook the garlic and ginger for a minute or two. Add the remaining vegetables, turn up the heat to medium-high and stir fry for a couple of minutes. Reduce the heat to medium, add the peanut sauce, cashews and tofu, and continue stir frying for a further 5 minutes.

4   Meanwhile, cook the noodles until al dente, then drain and add to the pan. Gently stir through to coat in the peanut sauce.

5   Divide between four bowls. Sprinkle on the garnish, and serve.

6   This dish is best eaten straight away. Leftovers can be refrigerated and eaten the next day, however the noodles may break up when reheated.

TIP When it comes to peanut butter, opt for a healthy brand that has no added oil, sugar or salt.

THE GOOD STUFF ♥
Broccoli is a good source of protein
and dietary fibre. It also has powerful
detoxifying and anti-inflammatory properties.
It is especially rich in vitamins K, C, A and
folate. Just half a cup of cooked broccoli
provides 138% of the vitamin K RDA and
84% of vitamin C.

Sweet 'n' Sour Stir Fry Noodles

Serves: 4   Hands on: 25 minutes   Ready in: 25 minutes

Home-made sweet 'n' sour sauce tastes so much fresher and 'real' compared to anything you can buy in a jar or from the Chinese take-away. By making this dish yourself, you can make sure it's packed with goodness, and doesn't include any dodgy additives like MSG or artificial colouring. This dish is easy to make from scratch and so quick that it will be on your table in less time than it takes to order and collect a take-away. Now that's my idea of the perfect 'fast food'!

1 TBSP olive oil

1 medium onion (130g), sliced

2-3 garlic cloves, minced

18g root ginger (1 inch piece), finely grated

1 medium carrot (100g), sliced into matchsticks (no need to peel organic carrots)

2 small bell peppers (300g), deseeded and sliced

2 medium tomatoes (200g), diced

100g / 1¼ cups mushrooms, chopped into chunks

½ medium head of broccoli (200g), cut into small florets

200g / 1 heaping cup fresh pineapple, cubed

40g / ¼ cup cashews

360ml / 1½ cups vegetable stock (broth)

3 TBSP apple cider vinegar

4 TBSP tomato ketchup

1½ TBSP unrefined sugar

1 TBSP cornflour (cornstarch)

160g / 1 heaping cup marinated or pan-fried tofu, cubed (p19) or substitute with another ¼ cup cashews

salt and ground black pepper, to taste

250g / 9 oz brown rice, whole wheat or other whole grain noodles

1   Prepare a large pan of boiling water for the noodles.

2   Heat the oil in a large wok or deep-sided frying pan (skillet) on medium heat. Stir fry the onion, garlic and ginger for 2 minutes. If it starts to stick, add a splash of water to loosen it. Add the remaining veggies, fruit and cashews. Continue stir frying for a couple of minutes.

3   Add the vegetable stock, vinegar, ketchup and sugar to the wok. Bring to the boil, then reduce the heat and simmer for 5 minutes.

4   Whisk the cornflour with 1 TBSP water until smooth, then add it to the wok along with the tofu. Continue cooking until the sauce has thickened slightly. Season with salt and black pepper. Taste test and add a touch more sweetener, if desired.

5   While the veggies are simmering, cook the noodles as per the instructions on the packet. Drain and return them to the pan. Add a few spoonfuls of the sweet 'n' sour sauce to the noodles and stir through.

6   Divide the noodles between four bowls. Spoon the stir fry on top and serve.

7   Any leftovers (excluding the noodles) can be stored in the refrigerator for five days, or for weeks in the freezer. If using store-bought marinated tofu, be sure to check the package for storage instructions.

Thai Coconut Curry

Serves: 4   Hands on: 20 minutes   Ready in: 20 minutes

Thai vegetable curries are one of my food passions. I love their vibrant colour, fragrant flavour and freshness. The veggies are barely cooked, so they retain their crisp textures and rich nutrients. Below I've listed the veggies that I typically use in this dish, but feel free to switch them up depending on what you have available. Baby corn, sugar snap peas and onion also work really well in this curry.

If serving to small children, I recommend making your own Thai curry paste (recipe overleaf). That way, you can adjust the heat levels to suit the family. It's really easy to make your own paste. It's simply a case of whizzing the ingredients together. The first time Lil' L tried this curry he absolutely loved it. Years later, it remains one of his all-time favourite dinners.

1 portion of home-made Thai Curry Paste (p111) or shop-bought Thai red curry paste suitable for vegetarians/vegans

400ml / 14 oz can coconut milk

1 red bell pepper (190g), deseeded and chopped

½ medium head of broccoli (220g), cut into small florets

½ medium head of cauliflower (300g), cut into small florets

1 medium carrot (100g), sliced into matchsticks (no need to peel organic carrots)

handful of curly kale leaves (35g), shredded, thick stalks removed

125g / 1¼ cups chestnut (or crimini) mushrooms, chopped into chunks

120ml / ½ cup water

1 TBSP tamari or reduced-salt soy sauce

½ tsp salt

2 dried kaffir lime leaves

50g / ¼ cup creamed coconut, finely chopped (see Tip on p120)

160g / 1 heaping cup pan-fried or marinated tofu, cubed (p19) or 110g / ¾ cup cashews (or use a mix of the two)

1   In a large heavy-bottomed pan, combine the spice paste with 3 TBSP coconut milk and gently cook for a couple of minutes. Stir in the remaining coconut milk, vegetables, water, soy sauce, salt, kaffir lime leaves and creamed coconut. Bring to the boil, then reduce the heat and simmer for 10 minutes or so, stirring now and then until the vegetables are crisp-tender. To begin with, it may look like you have too many veggies but they will reduce down.

2   When the curry is almost ready, stir in the tofu or cashews until warmed through. If you want to add more heat, first remove any children's portions then stir in some chopped red chilli. Remove the kaffir lime leaves before serving.

3   Any leftover curry can be stored in the refrigerator for up to five days or the freezer for weeks. If using store-bought marinated tofu, be sure to check the package for storage instructions.

Thai Curry Paste

Serves: 4   Hands on: 10 minutes   Ready in: 10 minutes

This paste can be used in our Thai Coconut Curry (p110), Malaysian Coconut Noodle Soup (p61) and Thai Sweet Potato Coconut Soup (p62). I make our pastes mild enough for children, but feel free to crank up the heat by adding extra chillies.

1 small red onion (100g), finely diced

1 red chilli (or more if you like it spicy), deseeded and finely chopped*

* If serving to children, use a mild chilli and remove the white membrane as this is where the heat is concentrated. Alternatively, add chilli to the curry once the children's portions have been served.

2-3 garlic cloves, minced

2 lemongrass stalks, trimmed and finely sliced

18g root ginger (1 inch piece), finely grated

1 tsp each ground cumin, ground coriander

1 TBSP fresh lime juice

1 tsp unrefined sugar

3 TBSP water

1   Place all the ingredients in a mini food processor (I use the bowl attachment that came with my hand blender). Add 3 TBSP water and blend into a coarse paste. Stop now and then to scrape down the sides.

2   The paste will keep for five days in the refrigerator. It also freezes well.

Caribbean Curry
with Fried Plantain

Serves: 4   Hands on: 30 minutes   Ready in: 30 minutes

Creamy, fruity, sunshine yellow and lightly spiced with a hint of rum. For me, this dish is full of the joys of the Caribbean. Millet is my favourite grain to serve with this curry. I find that its colour, flavour and texture are the perfect match.

2 TBSP olive oil, divided

1 ripe (yellow) plantain, sliced into coins (or substitute with 1 large unripe (green) banana)

1 large onion (160g), sliced

1 large red bell pepper (230g), deseeded and chopped

1 medium courgette (zucchini) (200g), quartered lengthwise and sliced into chunks

3 garlic cloves, minced

18g root ginger (1 inch piece), finely grated

1 tsp each ground coriander, ground cumin, ground cinnamon, mustard powder

½ tsp ground turmeric

¼ - ½ tsp cayenne pepper

400ml / 14 oz can coconut milk

juice of 1 lime

1 tsp unrefined sugar

190g / 1 heaping cup mango chunks, fresh or frozen

400g / 14 oz can pinto beans, drained

1-2 TBSP dark rum or banana liqueur (see Tip below)

salt, to taste

1   Heat 1 TBSP oil in a large non-stick frying pan (skillet) on medium heat. Fry the plantain/banana until browned on both sides, then tip onto a plate.

2   Add the remaining 1 TBSP oil to the pan and cook the onion, bell pepper and courgette for 3-4 minutes. Stir in the garlic and root ginger, and cook for another minute or so.

3   Add the spices and a couple of tablespoons of coconut milk to the pan and stir until fully combined. Add the remaining coconut milk along with the lime juice, sugar, mango, beans and rum. Bring to the boil then reduce the heat and simmer for 5 minutes. Season with salt, to taste.

4   Serve on a bed of grains, with slices of fried plantain/banana arranged on top.

5   Any leftover curry can be stored in the refrigerator for two days, or for weeks in the freezer. The sauce will thicken when chilled, but will thin out when reheated.

TIPS If serving to children, go for 1 TBSP rum or add the rum once their portion has been served. Most of the alcohol will burn off as it cooks so there's no chance of anyone getting tipsy.

Plantains can be tough to peel! To make it easier, first soak the plantain in hot water for 5-10 minutes to soften the skin. Slice off both ends, then slit down the skin lengthwise on two sides. It should now peel off with ease.

How to Cook Millet

Serves: 4   Hands on: 6 minutes   Ready in: 25 minutes

Millet has a mild nutty, corn flavour and a fluffy, slightly sticky texture that is not dissimilar to couscous. It's especially good for serving with 'saucy' dishes like stews and curries. When cooking millet, as a rule of thumb, I use double the volume of liquid to millet. It's important to cook at least 1 cup's worth of millet so there is sufficient water in the pan. Any less than this and the water may evaporate too quickly.

300g / 1⅓ cups millet   1 tsp olive oil
640ml / 2⅔ cups vegetable stock (broth)

1   To bring out its nutty flavour, first toast the millet in a saucepan over medium heat. Stir regularly and as soon as the seeds start to brown and become fragrant, pour in the stock. Bring to the boil then reduce the heat to low, cover with a tight-fitting lid and gently simmer for 15 minutes.

2   When air pockets have appeared in the millet and most of the water has been absorbed, it's ready. Remove from the heat and leave to stand, covered with a lid, for 5 minutes. Drizzle in the oil and fluff up with a fork before serving.

3   Stored in an airtight container, cooked millet will keep for up to five days in the refrigerator and a month in the freezer.

Spanish Veggie Paella

Serves: 4   Hands on: 15 minutes   Ready in: 30 minutes

When Lil' L was four years old, we went to stay on the beautiful island of Majorca. It was here that he had his first experience of paella. I'll never forget the shock on his face when he saw the enormous pans filled with mussels and crabs claws. He couldn't believe that people were actually going to eat them! Fortunately, the restaurant also had veggie paella on offer. It was absolutely delicious and the fresh veggies added beautiful, vibrant colours to the dish. Back home I couldn't wait to have a try at making my own paella. I discovered that it's really simple to make, requires very little preparation and only uses one pan. I love those types of meals!

This dish is one of the few occasions that I use refined rice rather than whole grain. For paella, you need a rice that absorbs a lot of water, plumps up and adds creaminess to the dish, and I'm yet to find a brown rice that does this. Most supermarkets stock Spanish paella rice but, if you can't find it, Arborio risotto rice is a good substitute. Saffron is the spice that gives paella its distinctive golden hue and nutty flavour. It is expensive though. For a budget-friendly alternative, a pinch of ground turmeric can be used instead.

1 TBSP olive oil

1 large onion (160g), finely diced

2-3 garlic cloves, minced

1 red bell pepper (200g), deseeded and diced

1 tsp each ground cumin, sweet paprika

300g / 1⅓ cups Spanish Paella rice

pinch of saffron (or substitute with ¼ tsp ground turmeric)

1 medium tomato (100g), diced

1 litre / 4 cups hot vegetable stock (broth)

handful of fresh or frozen fine green beans (about 100g), trimmed and halved

6-8 baby corn

80g / ½ cup cashews

salt, to taste

ground black or cayenne pepper, to taste

16 black pitted olives

sprinkling of nori flakes or dried parsley

35g / ⅓ cup toasted flaked almonds

1   Infuse the saffron in a little hot water and prepare the vegetable stock.

2   Gently heat the oil in a large deep-sided frying pan (skillet) and cook the onion until it starts to soften. Meanwhile, chop the remaining vegetables.

3   Add the garlic, bell pepper, cumin and paprika to the pan, and cook for a minute or so. If it starts to stick, add a splash of water to loosen it. Stir in the rice and saffron (or turmeric). Add the tomato and vegetable stock to the pan. Bring to the boil, then reduce the heat and simmer for 10 minutes uncovered.

4   Add the beans, baby corn and cashews, and cook for a further 10 minutes. Stir regularly towards the end of the cooking time. If the pan starts to dry out, add a little more stock or water.

5   While the rice is cooking, prepare any side dishes. We love to serve this paella with some Crispy Garlic Bread (p55) or Toasted Tortilla Chips (p53), and a large bowl of Crispy Kale (p184) to share.

6   When the rice is tender yet retains a bite, remove the pan from the heat. Season with salt and pepper to taste. Serve on warm plates with a sprinkling of olives, nori flakes/parsley and toasted flaked almonds.

7   Any leftovers can be stored in the refrigerator for 24 hours. As with any rice dish, make sure the leftover rice is cooled quickly and refrigerated within an hour.

Coconut Dhal with Butternut Squash

Serves: 4   Hands on: 15 minutes   Ready in: 35 minutes

With its mild taste and soft texture, dhal has got to be the most family-friendly Indian dish. It's also really easy to make and cheap too! I first introduced Lil' L to dhal when he was a toddler. As a twist on the classic recipe, and to bring a touch of sweetness and creaminess to the dish, I added some creamed coconut and butternut squash. He absolutely loved it and, to this day, it remains one of his favourite dishes. We love to serve it with chapattis (p119), which we roll and cook while the dhal is simmering.

1 TBSP olive oil

1 large onion (160g), finely diced

2-3 garlic cloves, minced

18g root ginger (1 inch piece), finely grated

2 tsp mustard seeds

1 tsp ground cumin

1 tsp garam masala

½ tsp ground turmeric

225g / 1¼ cups red lentils

800ml / 3½ cups vegetable stock (broth)

2 medium tomatoes (160g), diced

400g / 2½ cups butternut squash, diced

50g / ¼ cup creamed coconut, finely chopped (see Tip on p120)

salt, to taste

fresh coriander leaves (cilantro), for garnish

1   Place the lentils in a fine mesh sieve and wash under cold running water, agitating them with your hand until the water runs clear.

2   Gently heat the oil in a large heavy-bottomed saucepan and cook the onion until it starts to soften. Meanwhile, prepare the stock and remaining vegetables.

3   Add the garlic, ginger and dry spices to the pan, and cook on medium-low heat for 2 minutes. If it starts to stick to the pan, add a splash of water to loosen it. Add the lentils and stir through.

4   Add the stock, tomatoes, squash and creamed coconut. Bring to the boil then reduce the heat, cover with a lid, and simmer for 20 minutes. Stir towards the end of the cooking time and add a splash of extra stock or water, if needed. When the lentils are tender, remove the pan from the heat and leave to rest for a couple of minutes. Season with salt, to taste.

5   This dish is delicious served with flatbreads (home-made chapattis or soft flour tortillas), brown rice or both! Any leftover dhal can be stored for up to five days in the refrigerator or for weeks in the freezer.

THE GOOD STUFF ♥

Lentils are an excellent source of protein and dietary fibre,
providing slow release energy and helping to regulate blood
sugar levels. They are rich in antioxidant phytonutrients,
B vitamins and minerals. One cup of cooked lentils provides
over one third of the recommended daily amount of iron.

How to Cook Brown Rice using the Absorption Method

Serves: 4   Hands on: 5 minutes   Ready in: 35 minutes

I find the following method cooks brown rice to perfection. As a rule of thumb, I use double the volume of water to rice. It's important to cook at least 1 cup's worth of rice so that there is sufficient water in the pan. Any less than this and the water will evaporate too quickly.

265g / 1⅓ cups easy cook brown rice   640g / 2⅔ cups water

Place the rice in a fine mesh sieve and rinse under running cold water. Place the rice in a heavy-bottomed saucepan along with the water. Bring to the boil, then reduce the heat and simmer uncovered for 10 minutes. Reduce the heat to low, cover with a tight-fitting lid, and cook for a further 20 minutes. When air pockets have appeared in the rice, it's ready. Remove from the heat and leave to rest for 5 minutes, covered with the lid, then serve.

TIP Harmful bacteria that causes food poisoning can grow on rice that is left standing at room temperature for too long. The UK National Health Service (NHS) recommends that leftover rice be cooled quickly and refrigerated within an hour of being cooked. Consume the rice within 24 hours, and make sure it is thoroughly heated through before serving. Never reheat rice more than once.

THE GOOD STUFF ♥

Brown rice is high in dietary fibre, B vitamins and a whole host of minerals including manganese, selenium, magnesium, phosphorus and copper. When brown rice is milled into white rice, the majority of its dietary fibre, vitamins and minerals are lost.

Chapattis

Serves: 4   Hands on: 30 minutes   Ready in: 30 minutes

Chapattis are traditionally made with atta (chapatti) flour, which is a very fine wholemeal (whole wheat) flour. It can be found in the world food aisle of larger supermarkets or in Indian food stores. I love the fine texture of chapatti flour and find it perfect for baking. As well as flat breads, it's my favourite flour for cakes, cookies and pizza crusts.

> 280g / 2 cups chapatti flour (or substitute with 140g / 1 cup fine wholemeal (whole wheat pastry) flour and 140g /1 cup plain (all purpose) flour)
> ½ tsp salt
> 180ml / ¾ cup non-dairy milk

1   Place the flour and salt in a large bowl. Make a well in the centre. Slowly stir in the milk with a fork until it starts to come together, then continue to form into a dough with your hand. (Depending on the type of flour you use, you may not need all the milk). Turn out the dough onto a lightly floured surface and knead until smooth and elastic.

2   Divide the dough into eight balls (I weigh my dough to divide it evenly). Lightly coat a ball in flour and roll into a thin circle about 20cm / 8 inches in diameter. Place on a plate and lay a piece of kitchen paper towel on top (this prevents the chapattis sticking together). Repeat the process with the remaining dough.

3   Heat a frying pan (skillet) on medium-high. Using no oil, cook a chapatti on one side for about 30 seconds, or until brown spots appear on the underside. Flip over and cook until brown spots appear on the second side (about 15 seconds). Flip over one more time and cook for a few more seconds (the chapatti should start to puff up). Place the chapatti on a plate with a sheet of kitchen paper towel on top (this will absorb the steam and enable the chapattis to be stacked). Repeat the process with the remaining dough balls.

4   Chapattis are best served immediately, however they will last a couple of days in an airtight container in the refrigerator. To refresh them, sprinkle lightly with water and gently heat them through in the oven.

Indian-Spiced Sweet Potato Curry

Serves: 4-5   Hands on: 20 minutes   Ready in: 35 minutes

With its sweet, mildly-spiced flavour and soft, creamy texture, this curry is perfect for all the family. As a mid-week meal, we serve it with a side dish of brown rice. For a full-blown Indian feast - perfect for special weekend meals and dinner parties - we add a pile of freshly made chapattis (p119) and a starter of poppadoms, onion bhajis (p86) and mango chutney (p87).

1 TBSP olive oil	750ml / 3 cups vegetable stock (broth)
1 large onion (160g), diced	1 large tomato (125g), diced
3 medium sweet potatoes (500g), scrubbed and cut into bite-size chunks (peeling is optional)	50g / ¼ cup creamed coconut, finely chopped (see Tip below)
140g / ¾ cup red lentils	2 handfuls of spinach leaves (80g), roughly chopped
1 portion of home-made Indian curry paste (overleaf) or 2 TBSP shop-bought paste (use mild curry or korma paste for children)	sprinkling of toasted flaked almonds and sesame seeds, for garnish

1   Heat the oil in a large heavy-bottomed pan and cook the onion and sweet potato on medium-low heat for about 6 minutes, stirring occasionally.

2   Meanwhile, place the lentils in a fine mesh sieve and rinse under cold running water, agitating with your hand until the water runs clear.

3   Add the curry paste to the pan, and cook for a couple of minutes. Add a touch of water, if needed, to loosen the mixture. Stir in the lentils until coated in curry paste. Add the stock, tomato and creamed coconut. Bring to the boil, then reduce the heat and simmer, uncovered, for 15 minutes. When the potato and lentils are tender, stir in the spinach and continue cooking until it has wilted.

4   Remove the curry from the heat and leave to rest for a couple of minutes. Taste test and adjust the seasoning to suit. Sprinkle on the garnish and serve.

5   Any leftover curry can be stored in the refrigerator for five days, or for weeks in the freezer.

TIP Sometimes a block of creamed coconut can have a layer of coconut oil in it. It's easy to spot as it's bright white in colour. In curries, use only the opaque cream-coloured section of the block. The coconut oil can be saved for other recipes. For more information on creamed coconut, see p11.

Indian Curry Paste

Serves: 4-5   Hands on: 5 minutes   Ready in: 5 minutes

It's so easy to make Indian curry pastes from scratch. It's literally a case of whizzing the ingredients together. It also gives you the flexibility to adjust the heat levels to suit your family's tastes. The recipe below is for a mild paste (suitable for children) but feel free to crank up the heat by adding some chillies or hot curry powder.

1 small onion (100g), diced
18g root ginger (1 inch piece), finely grated
2 garlic cloves, minced
2 TBSP tomato purée (paste)
2 tsp curry powder (use mild for children)

1 tsp ground coriander
1 tsp ground cumin
½ tsp ground turmeric
½ tsp sweet paprika
¼ tsp salt
3 TBSP water

1   Place all the ingredients in a small food processor (I use the bowl attachment that came with my hand blender) and blitz into a coarse paste.

2   Stored in an airtight container in the refrigerator, this paste will keep for a week. It is also freezable.

Easy Peasy Burgers

Serves: 4   Hands on: 30 minutes   Ready in: 30 minutes

Here I present to you one of our all-time favourite veggie burgers – the Black Eye Bean Burger. One summer, we invited friends to join us for a BBQ. They brought their meat burgers and I made a batch of these bean burgers. One friend was intrigued to taste the bean burger and declared it to be delicious. Word then spread and, before I knew it, all the bean burgers were gone and we were left with a big pile of meat burgers. So there we have it, a great tasting veggie burger, approved by meat eaters and sturdy enough to withstand barbecuing. It's a winner!

1 TBSP olive oil, divided

1 medium onion (130g), finely diced

70g / 1 cup mushrooms, finely diced

2-3 garlic cloves, minced

1 tsp paprika

1 tsp ground cumin

½ tsp cayenne pepper

1 tsp Dijon mustard

2 TBSP natural peanut butter

1 TBSP tahini

400g / 14 oz can black eye beans (aka black eyed peas), thoroughly drained

50g / ½ cup rolled oats (quick oats, not jumbo)

½ tsp salt

1 TBSP fresh parsley, finely chopped

1   Heat ½ TBSP oil in a large non-stick frying pan (skillet). Add the onions and mushrooms and cook on medium heat for 5 minutes.

2   Add the garlic and spices to the pan, and continue cooking until the liquid from the mushrooms has evaporated. Stir in the mustard, peanut butter and tahini, then remove from the heat.

3   Place the beans in a fine mesh sieve. Rinse under cold water then shake to remove all the water droplets. Tip the beans into a large bowl and roughly mash using a potato masher. Stir in the rolled oats.

4   Add the contents of the frying pan to the bowl, along with the salt and parsley. Stir with a wooden spoon until the mixture is thoroughly combined. Taste the mixture and adjust the seasoning, if desired.

5   Divide the mixture into four equal size balls. Firmly press the mixture together, then shape into patties.

6   Coat the bottom of the frying pan with the remaining oil and cook the burgers on medium-low heat for 6 minutes on each side, or until browned.

7   We love to serve these burgers in toasted buns with salad, slices of avocado and sweet pickle or caramelised onion chutney, and a big bowl of Crispy Kale (p184) to share.

8   These burgers can be stored in the refrigerator for two days. They also freeze really well.

THE GOOD STUFF ♥
Like all legumes, black eye beans are a great source of protein, dietary fibre, antioxidant phytonutrients, B vitamins and minerals. One cup of cooked black eye beans contains 27% of the protein RDA, 45% of dietary fibre and 24% of iron.

Gourmet Goa Burgers

Serves: 4   Hands on: 25 minutes   Ready in: 25 minutes

Once you've had a taste of home-made burgers, you'll never want to go back to the store-bought version. They taste so much fresher, the texture is way nicer and they're really easy to prepare. Indian, Thai, Moroccan, Smoky BBQ - the flavour options are endless. This colourful Indian-spiced burger is a firm family favourite.

1 TBSP olive oil, divided

1 medium red onion (130g), finely diced

2-3 garlic cloves, minced

1-2 tsp curry powder (use mild for children)

1 TBSP natural peanut butter

75g / ½ cup cashews

400g / 14 oz can kidney beans, thoroughly drained

50g / ½ cup rolled oats (quick oats, not jumbo)

2 TBSP fresh coriander leaves (cilantro), roughly chopped

½ tsp salt

1   Gently heat ½ TBSP oil in a large non-stick frying pan (skillet) and cook the onion for 4 minutes. Add the garlic and curry powder and cook for another minute. Stir in the peanut butter then remove the pan from the heat.

2   Roughly chop the nuts either using a knife with a curved blade or by whizzing them in a food processor.

3   Place the beans in a mesh sieve. Rinse under cold water then shake to remove all the water droplets.

4   Tip the beans into a large mixing bowl and roughly mash using a potato masher. Add the contents of the frying pan, along with the chopped nuts, oats, coriander leaves and salt. Stir until thoroughly combined. Taste the burger mixture and adjust the seasoning to suit.

5   Divide the mixture into four equal size balls. Firmly press the mixture together, then shape into patties.

6   Coat the bottom of the frying pan with the remaining oil and cook the burgers on medium-low heat for 6 minutes on each side, or until browned.

7   We love to serve these burgers in toasted buns with colourful salad leaves, slices of avocado and a generous spoonful of sweet pickle or home-made mango chutney (p87).

8   Stored in an airtight container, the burgers will keep for two days in the refrigerator. They also freeze well.

Bean Enchiladas
with Roasted Butternut Squash

Serves: 4   Hands on: 30 minutes   Ready in: 40 minutes

While I love Mexican food, even the mild dishes in Mexican restaurants can leave me red faced and feeling like my mouth's on fire (yes, I know, I'm a wimp!) The great thing about making home-cooked Mexican food is that you can customise the level of heat to suit individual tastes. I've made our enchiladas mild enough for children (and spice wimps like me!) but once you've served any children's portions, feel free to crank up the heat by adding more chilli or cayenne pepper.

1½ TBSP olive oil, divided

600g / 4½ cups butternut squash, sliced into small bite-size pieces

1 large onion (170g), finely diced

1 red bell pepper (190g), deseeded and finely diced

2-3 garlic cloves, minced

2 tsp dried oregano

1 tsp smoked paprika

½ tsp chilli powder (use mild chilli for children)

2 TBSP tomato purée (paste)

400g / 14 oz can chopped tomatoes

120ml / ½ cup vegetable stock (broth)

1 tsp unrefined sugar

½ tsp salt

400g / 14 oz can black beans, rinsed and drained

400g / 14 oz can pinto beans, rinsed and drained

sweet chilli sauce, optional

cayenne pepper, optional

4 large whole grain or seeded soft tortillas (use GF tortillas, if needed)

Topping

4 heaping TBSP non-dairy natural yogurt

1 avocado, finely diced

small handful of fresh coriander leaves (cilantro)

1   Preheat the oven to 200C (180C fan) / 400F.

2   Tip the squash into a large roasting tin. Drizzle in 1 TBSP oil and stir through. Roast for 30 minutes, or until tender. Stir halfway through the cooking time.

3   Heat ½ TBSP oil in a large frying pan (skillet) and cook the onion and bell pepper on medium heat for 4 minutes. Add the garlic, oregano, paprika and chilli powder, and cook for a further minute.

4   Add the tomato purée, chopped tomatoes, vegetable stock, sugar and salt to the pan. Bring to the boil then reduce the heat and simmer, uncovered, for 10 minutes.

5   Transfer about a third of the contents of the frying pan into a jug and set to one side (this will be used for topping the enchiladas).

6   Add the beans and roasted squash to the frying pan and stir through to combine. Cook for a few minutes until piping hot. If you'd like to spice up your enchiladas, first remove any children's portions, then add some chilli sauce or cayenne pepper.

7   Warm the tortilla wraps for a few seconds in the oven to soften them, then fill and fold them up to make fat parcels. Place in the roasting tin, seam side down. Drizzle the remaining tomato mixture across the centre of the enchiladas.

8   Grill (broil) until the edges of the enchiladas are browned (keep a close eye on them). Add the toppings and serve immediately. A colourful baby leaf salad makes a great accompaniment to this dish. Any leftover filling can be stored in the refrigerator for two days, or for weeks in the freezer.

Rainbow Veggie Chilli

Serves: 4   Hands on: 20 minutes   Ready in: 55 minutes

Mexican chilli is one of our favourite cold season dishes. I love to fill our chillies with colourful, nutrient-packed, flavourful veggies that stimulate our senses and brighten up the dark, winter evenings. Just seeing all those colours is enough to put a big smile on my face. We love to serve this chilli with a wedge or two of home-made cornbread (p54), which adds even more colour to the plate. The cornbread can be prepared while the chilli is simmering.

1 TBSP olive oil

1 medium onion (130g), finely diced

2-3 garlic cloves, minced

1 medium bell pepper (200g) deseeded and diced (or use a mix of red, yellow, green pepper pieces for extra colour)

1 medium carrot (90g), quartered lengthwise and thinly sliced

½ medium courgette (zucchini) (100g), quartered lengthwise and sliced

2 tsp dried oregano

1 tsp smoked paprika

chilli powder, to taste (use ½ tsp mild chilli for children)

85g / ½ cup sweetcorn

125g / 1½ cups mushrooms, diced

400g / 14 oz can kidney or pinto beans, rinsed and drained

180g / 2 cups meat-free mince or 400g / 14 oz can black beans, rinsed and drained

400g / 14 oz can chopped tomatoes

120ml / ½ cup vegetable stock (broth)

2 TBSP tomato purée (paste)

1 tsp unrefined sugar

½ tsp salt

1   Gently heat the oil in a large heavy-bottomed saucepan and cook the onion until it starts to soften. Meanwhile, chop the remaining veggies.

2   Add the garlic, bell pepper, carrot, courgette, oregano, paprika and chilli powder to the pan, and cook for a couple of minutes. If serving to children, begin by adding ½ tsp mild chilli powder.

3   Stir in the remaining ingredients. Bring to the boil then reduce the heat, partially cover with a lid and simmer for about 30 minutes, or until the carrot is tender.

4   When the veggies are cooked through, remove any children's portions and add more chilli powder, to taste.

5   Leftover chilli will keep for a couple of days in the refrigerator. It also freezes well.
If using meat-free mince, be sure to check the storage instructions on the packet.

THE GOOD STUFF ♥

Bell peppers (aka capsicum) are packed with antioxidants. Red peppers are the most nutrient-dense, containing nine times as much betacarotene compared to green peppers. Just one cup of chopped red pepper contains over 300% of the vitamin C RDA and almost 100% of vitamin A.

Butternut Squash & Apricot Tagine

Serves: 6   Hands on: 30 minutes   Ready in: 60 minutes

I had my first tagine experience in Istanbul. I adored the aromatic flavour of the sauce and the combination of tender vegetables and sweet dried fruits. Back home, I couldn't wait to experiment with different vegetables, fruits and legumes to produce my own tagines. The Moroccan-inspired recipe below is one of the family's favourites. This tagine can easily be prepared in advance. Simply heat through on the stove before serving.

1 TBSP olive oil

1 large onion (170g), finely diced

2 celery sticks (140g), diced

2-3 garlic cloves, minced

1 tsp each ground ginger, ground cinnamon, ground cumin

360g / 2½ cups butternut squash, cut into bite-size pieces

pinch of saffron, optional but highly recommended

400g / 14 oz can chopped tomatoes

240ml / 1 cup vegetable stock (broth)

2 TBSP tomato purée (paste)

400g / 14 oz can chickpeas, drained

100g / 2 packed cups spinach leaves, finely chopped

16 dried apricots, halved

1½ TBSP maple syrup

½ tsp salt

½ - 1 TBSP Harissa paste, optional

Garnish

handful of toasted flaked almonds and toasted sesame seeds

small handful of fresh coriander leaves (cilantro), roughly chopped

1   Gently heat the oil in a large heavy-bottomed saucepan or casserole and cook the onion and celery until they start to soften. Meanwhile, prepare the remaining vegetables.

2   Stir in the garlic, spices and butternut squash. If it starts to stick to the pan, add a splash of water to loosen it. Cover with a lid and leave to sweat on low heat for 5 minutes.

3   Meanwhile, steep the saffron in a little hot water. Add the saffron (liquid and strands) and all the remaining tagine ingredients to the pan and stir through. Bring to the boil then reduce the heat, cover with a lid and simmer for 40 minutes, or until the squash has a soft 'melt in your mouth' texture.

4   If you wish to add a spicy kick to the dish, first remove any children's portions then stir in some Harissa paste.

5   When the tagine is ready, serve in warm bowls on a bed of couscous (or gluten-free grain such as rice or millet). Sprinkle on the garnish and serve.

6   Any leftover tagine can be stored in an airtight container in the refrigerator for a couple of days, or for weeks in the freezer.

THE GOOD STUFF ♥
Butternut squash is rich in vitamin A antioxidants alphacarotene and betacarotene. It also provides the highest amount of vitamin C out of all the winter squashes. Just one cup of cooked squash provides 457% of the recommended daily amount of vitamin A and 52% of vitamin C.

Mediterranean Savoury Crumble

Serves: 4   Hands on: 25 minutes   Ready in: 60 minutes

Most people associate crumble with fruity desserts but by switching a couple of ingredients, it transforms into the perfect topping for a savoury dish. Bean casseroles aren't usually popular with children, but top it with crumble and watch how they scoff it down! When Lil' L was a toddler, I used to roughly blend the veggies into the sauce before adding the beans. These days, he's more than happy to eat the 'grown up' version. As a main meal, we love to serve this casserole freshly baked, with slices of Crispy Garlic Bread (p55). It can also be served cold, and any leftovers make a great addition to lunchboxes.

Casserole

½ TBSP olive oil

1 large onion (170g), finely diced

2 celery sticks (130g), finely diced

2-3 garlic cloves, minced

1 sweet romano or red bell pepper (190g), deseeded and diced

1 medium courgette (zucchini) (200g), diced

125g / 1¼ cups mushrooms, finely diced

3 tsp Italian mixed herbs (I use oregano, sage, thyme)

1 tsp smoked paprika

400g / 14 oz can borlotti beans, drained

400g / 14 oz can chopped tomatoes

2 TBSP tomato purée (paste)

1-2 tsp unrefined sugar

½ tsp salt

2 TBSP sunflower seeds

Crumble

70g / ½ cup fine wholemeal (whole wheat pastry) flour, chapatti flour or GF flour mix

70g / ¾ cup rolled oats (quick oats, not jumbo)

1 tsp mustard powder

2 TBSP nutritional yeast flakes, optional

pinch of salt

80g / ⅓ cup dairy-free spread/ vegan butter

27g / ¼ cup flaked almonds

1   Gently heat the oil in a large heavy-bottomed saucepan. Cook the onion and celery until they start to soften. Meanwhile, prepare the remaining vegetables.

2   Stir in the garlic, red pepper, courgette, mushrooms, Italian herbs and smoked paprika. Reduce the heat to low, cover with a lid, and leave to sweat for 5-10 minutes.

3   Add the beans, chopped tomatoes, tomato purée, sugar, salt and sunflower seeds to the pan. Bring to the boil then reduce the heat, cover with a lid and simmer for 15 minutes. Taste test and adjust the seasoning to suit.

4   Preheat the oven to 190C (170C fan) / 375 F.

THE GOOD STUFF ♥
Tomatoes are packed with antioxidants, including vitamin C, betacarotene, lutein, quercetin and lycopene. Cooked tomatoes contain more lycopene than raw tomatoes. Since lycopene is fat soluble, it helps to cook them in a little oil.

5 To prepare the crumble, place the flour, oats, mustard powder, nutritional yeast, salt and dairy-free spread/vegan butter in a food processor and pulse until the mixture starts to come together to form coarse, chunky crumbs (don't overprocess). Add the almonds and pulse a couple of times to combine.

6 Tip the vegetables and beans into a 2 litre / 2 quart ovenproof dish (about 21cm x 21cm x 6cm / 8" x 8" x 2½" in size). Sprinkle the crumble evenly on top. Bake for 20 minutes, until the sauce is bubbling and the almonds are lightly browned. Leave to rest for a couple of minutes before serving.

7 Stored in an airtight container, the crumble will keep for a couple of days in the refrigerator. It also freezes well.

Sweet Chestnut Casserole
with Herby Dumplings

Serves: 4   Hands on: 30 minutes   Ready in: 1 hour

For me, a forest floor littered with prickly chestnut cases signals the start of another beautiful season. As soon as autumn arrives, we love to take a trip to Sherwood Forest where we ride our bikes, lark about shooting arrows pretending we're part of Robin Hood's merry gang, and forage for sweet chestnuts. Back home, my favourite way to serve chestnuts is in a warming casserole topped with herby dumplings. This is comfort food at its best.

Casserole

1 TBSP olive oil

1 medium onion (130g), finely diced

2 celery sticks (130g), finely diced

1 large sweet potato (400g) peeled and chopped into small bite-size pieces

2 medium carrots (150g), sliced into thin disks

200g / 2½ cups chestnut (or crimini) mushrooms, diced

1 tsp each dried rosemary, sage, thyme

1 tsp sweet paprika

480ml / 2 cups vegetable stock (broth)

2 TBSP tomato purée (paste)

180g / 1 heaping cup cooked (ready to eat) chestnuts (e.g. Merchant Gourmet)

3 TBSP mixed seeds (e.g. sunflower, pumpkin, shelled hemp seeds)

1 TBSP cornflour (cornstarch)

salt and ground black pepper, to taste

Dumplings

90g / ⅔ cup fine wholemeal (whole wheat pastry) flour or chapatti flour

90g / ⅔ cup plain (all purpose) flour

1 TBSP baking powder

2 tsp dried rosemary

1 tsp dried parsley

1 tsp mustard powder

½ tsp salt

40ml / 3 TBSP olive oil

80ml / ⅓ cup soya milk

1   Gently heat the oil in a large casserole or heavy-bottomed pan. Add the vegetables, dried herbs and paprika. Cover with a lid and leave to sweat for 5 minutes. Stir in the vegetable stock and tomato purée. (To begin with, it may look like you have too many vegetables, but they will reduce down). Bring to the boil then reduce the heat, cover with a lid and simmer for 10 minutes, stirring occasionally.

2   Meanwhile, prepare the dumplings: Place the flours, baking powder, herbs, mustard powder and salt in a bowl and mix well. Add the oil and milk, and stir with a fork until it starts to come together. Finish bringing the dough together by hand. It should be a soft, slightly sticky dough, so add a touch more liquid or flour if needed to attain the right consistency. Divide the mixture into 12-16 equal pieces and roll into balls.

3   Slice the chestnuts in half and add them to the casserole, along with the seeds. Mix the cornflour with 1 TBSP water until smooth, then stir it into the casserole. Add salt and pepper, to taste. Arrange the dumplings on top, cover with a lid and simmer for 15 minutes.

4   Ladle into warm bowls and serve. Any leftovers can be stored in the refrigerator for three days.

GLUTEN FREE OPTION ♥
For a delicious gluten-free
alternative to dumplings,
serve the casserole on a
bed of root vegetable and
potato mash.

Mediterranean Deep Crust Pizza

Serves: 2-3   Hands on: 20 minutes   Ready in: 1 hour 40 minutes

SPEEDY PIZZA & GF OPTIONS ♥

For a super quick pizza, use a shop-bought pizza base. We especially love the wood-fired or stone-baked bases. Gluten-free pizza bases are available in the UK from health food stores and the 'Free From' aisle in major supermarkets. America's famous Venice Bakery gluten-free pizza bases are available to purchase in the UK online.

'Healthy' and 'Pizza' are not words that you normally see written together but all that is about to change! With a wholemeal crust and abundance of veggies, this Mediterranean pizza is positively brimming with the good stuff. I add semolina into the pizza crust as I love the flavour and texture it provides. If semolina is unavailable, you can substitute with plain (all purpose) flour instead.

Pizza dough

210g / 1½ cups fine wholemeal (whole wheat pastry) flour or chapatti flour

90g / ½ cup semolina or 90g / ½ packed cup plain (all purpose) flour

½ tsp fast action yeast

¾ tsp salt

1 tsp sugar

1 TBSP extra virgin olive oil

170ml / scant ¾ cup lukewarm water

Topping

3-4 TBSP sun-dried tomato paste or pesto

6 sun-dried tomatoes in olive oil, drained and diced

1 small red onion (80g), sliced

¼ medium courgette (zucchini) (50g), sliced into thin strips

½ red bell pepper (90g), deseeded and sliced

2-3 mushrooms, thinly sliced

1 TBSP pine nuts

1 tsp dried oregano

pinch of salt

sprinkling of nutritional yeast flakes

olive oil, for drizzling (I use the oil from the sun-dried tomato jar)

1   - In a bread maker: Place all the dough ingredients in the machine and select the 'pizza' setting. Once ready, leave to rest for 20 minutes or so.

- Or by hand: Place the flour, semolina, yeast, salt and sugar in a large bowl. Make a well in the middle and pour in the oil and water. Stir with a fork until it starts to come together, then work into a dough with your hands. Turn out onto a floured surface and knead for 10 minutes. Place the dough in a clean, lightly oiled bowl. Cover with a damp tea towel and leave in a warm place for an hour or so to prove. (Since the dough contains wholemeal flour it won't rise much, but this is okay).

2   When ready to prepare the pizza, preheat the oven to 220C (200C fan) / 425F.

3   Tip the dough onto a surface lightly dusted with flour. Roll into a circle about 25cm / 10 inches in diameter. Transfer the pizza to a lightly oiled pizza tray or non-stick baking sheet. Work your way round the pizza, folding over the edge and pressing down to form a raised crust.

4   Spread the sun-dried tomato paste over the dough and add the toppings. (Be generous with the veggies as they shrink on cooking). Sprinkle on the nuts, oregano, salt, nutritional yeast and a light drizzle of oil. Bake in the preheated oven for 15-20 minutes, until the centre of the pizza is cooked through.

5   We love to serve this pizza straight from the oven, with a side dish of colourful salad leaves and olives. It can also be eaten cold and any leftovers make a great addition to lunchboxes. It will keep for three days in the refrigerator.

THE GOOD STUFF ♥

Spinach is packed with antioxidant phytonutrients including betacarotene, lutein and zeaxanthin, which have powerful anti-inflammatory and disease-fighting properties. Just half a cup of cooked spinach contains 188% of the vitamin A RDA and 555% of vitamin K.

Spinach & Tofu 'Ricotta' Pie

Serves: 4   Hands on: 30 minutes   Ready in: 65 minutes

When Lil' L was a baby, one of the first savoury foods I fed him was the filling from this pie. He absolutely loved it! To this day, it remains one of his favourite dinners. As a main meal, we love to serve it straight from the oven with a side helping of new potatoes and mixed salad. The tofu 'ricotta' also works really well in pasta dishes such as lasagne and cannelloni, or for filling large pasta shells.

olive oil
2 medium onions (260g), finely diced
2-3 garlic cloves, minced
200g / 4 packed cups fresh spinach leaves
400g / 14 oz firm tofu
1 tsp Dijon mustard

1 small handful of fresh basil leaves, chopped
1 tsp dried oregano
2 TBSP nutritional yeast flakes
½ tsp salt
2 TBSP pine nuts
6 sheets of filo pastry

1   Preheat the oven to 190C (170C fan) / 375F. Lightly oil a 1.5 litre / 1½ quart ovenproof dish (about 17cm x 22cm x 6cm / 7" x 9" x 2½").

2   Gently heat ½ TBSP oil in a non-stick frying pan (skillet) and cook the onion and garlic for 3-4 minutes.

3   Place the spinach in a strainer over the sink and pour boiling water on top until it starts to wilt. Run under cold water to cool it down, then squeeze hard to remove the water. Roughly chop the spinach.

4   Drain the tofu and squeeze to remove as much water as possible.

5   Crumble the tofu into a food processor (or use a large bowl and hand blender). Add the spinach, mustard, basil and 1 tsp olive oil, and blend smooth. Add the onion, garlic, oregano, nutritional yeast and salt, and pulse to combine. Stir in the pine nuts.

6   Cover the filo sheets with a damp tea cloth to prevent them drying out. Lay one sheet on a clean work surface and lightly brush with oil. Lay another sheet directly on top. Place the two sheets in the dish so that they cover the bottom and overhang two sides. Repeat with another two filo sheets. Spoon the spinach ricotta into the dish.

7   Lightly brush the remaining two filo sheets with oil, crinkle them up and place on top of the pie. Fold up the edges overhanging the dish onto the pie. Brush the top of the pie with oil and pierce a couple of times to allow the steam to escape. Bake in the preheated oven for 30 minutes or until golden brown.

8   The pie is best served immediately while it's warm and crispy. It can be eaten cold though and any leftover pie makes a tasty treat for lunchboxes. Stored in an airtight container, it will keep for two days in the refrigerator.

Cranberry-Glazed Nut Loaf

Serves: 6   Hands on: 30 minutes   Ready in: 1 hour 50 minutes

This nut loaf is perfect for sharing with friends and family over the festive holidays or as a special Sunday roast dinner. It can easily be made in advance and stores very well. Dressing it up with a cranberry glaze makes it an attractive centrepiece for Christmas and Thanksgiving dinners, plus it tastes really yummy! This loaf has proven to be a huge hit with my readers. To this day, it remains one of the most popular recipes on my blog.

225g / 1½ cups cashews

125g / 4½ oz fresh wholemeal bread or 2 cups breadcrumbs

200g / 1 cup red lentils

500ml / 2 cups vegetable stock (broth)

1 TBSP olive oil

1 large red onion (160g), finely diced

2 celery sticks (140g), finely diced

2-3 garlic cloves, minced

100g / 1 cup mushrooms, finely diced

1 tsp dried sage

2 TBSP tomato purée (paste)

40g / ⅓ cup wholemeal (whole wheat) flour

2-3 TBSP fresh parsley, finely chopped

½ tsp salt

1 TBSP each of pine nuts, pumpkin seeds and sunflower seeds

4 TBSP cranberry sauce

1   Preheat the oven to 190C (170C fan) / 375F. Grease the sides of a large (3lb) loaf tin (about 24cm x 13cm x 7cm / 9½" x 5" x 3" in size) and line with non-stick baking paper to cover the bottom and long sides. Leave some paper hanging over the sides to make it easy to lift out.

2   Pulse the cashews in a food processor until coarsely chopped, then place in a large mixing bowl. Process the bread into breadcrumbs, then add to the mixing bowl.

3   Place the lentils in a fine mesh sieve and wash under cold running water, agitating them with your hand until the water runs clear.

4   In a saucepan, bring the vegetable stock and lentils to the boil, then reduce the heat and gently simmer uncovered for 15 minutes, or until the lentils have become a soft purée and all the water has been absorbed. Stir regularly, especially towards the end of the cooking time to prevent the lentils from sticking.

5   Meanwhile, heat the oil in a large non-stick frying pan (skillet) and cook the onion and celery on medium-low heat for 5 minutes. Add the garlic, mushrooms and sage, and cook for a further 3 minutes. Stir in the tomato purée and flour, then remove from the heat.

6   Add the contents of the frying pan to the mixing bowl with the cashews and breadcrumbs. Add the cooked lentils, parsley and salt, and stir until thoroughly combined.

7   Spoon the mixture into the prepared tin. Press down and level the top. Sprinkle with pine nuts and seeds, and press them into the loaf. Spread the cranberry sauce on top. Cover with foil and bake for 30 minutes. Remove the foil and bake for a further 30 minutes.

8   Leave to cool in the tin for at least 20 minutes before turning out and slicing (it will firm up as it cools). This loaf will keep for five days in the refrigerator, and for weeks in the freezer. It can be served hot or cold. It also makes a great sandwich filling (p71).

Red Onion Miso Gravy

Yield: about 400ml / 1 3/4 cups   Hands on: 8 minutes   Ready in: 30 minutes

This is my favourite gravy for serving with roast dinners. It's really easy to make and so flavourful!

1 large red onion (210g)
480ml / 2 cups vegetable stock (broth)
2 TBSP white miso

1 TBSP tamari or reduced-salt soy sauce
2 tsp cornflour (cornstarch) dissolved in
1 TBSP water, optional

1   Slice the onion into chunks. Add it to a saucepan along with the vegetable stock. Bring to the boil then reduce the heat and simmer until the onion is soft (about 10 minutes). Stir in the white miso and soy sauce. Leave to cool slightly then blend smooth using a hand or jug blender.

2   If you wish to thicken the gravy, pour the cornflour paste into the gravy. Bring to the boil then reduce the heat and simmer, stirring continuously until the gravy reaches the desired consistency.

Desserts, Treats & Snacks

This chapter begins with speedy desserts (perfect for busy weekdays) followed by a couple of my favourite special desserts. Unlike traditional British desserts, these ones are packed with goodness. They will energise you and make you feel fantastic on the inside. These are the kinds of desserts that you can enjoy every day and I wholeheartedly encourage you to do so!

After desserts, we have a compilation of popular treats, including cakes, cookies and chocolates. As a finale, I share some of my family's favourite sweet and savoury snacks. We love them and hope you do too!

Goji Yogi Surprise

Serves: 2   Hands on: 5 minutes   Ready in: 5 minutes

As a youngster, Lil' L was not a fan of fruit. It seemed to be more of a texture issue than flavour, but his dislike of fruits spanned almost the whole food group. He would begrudgingly eat a couple of slices of apple or banana then ask me what he was having for his 'real' dessert. For him, the after dinner fruit course was a chore that he had to get through before he could have his 'proper' dessert. I realised I needed to get creative. Rather than simply presenting him with a slice of fruit, I needed to dress it up a little, make it more special. I wanted him to see fruit eating as a pleasure, something to be enjoyed rather than endured.

One of my first successes was this 'Goji Yogi Surprise' (a title chosen by one of my lovely blog readers). The surprise being that it contains a whole apple puréed into a smooth sauce, layered between yogurt and topped with a sprinkling of goji berries, nuts and granola. It only took a couple of minutes to make but Lil' L loved it. What a transformation! And all it took was a little creativity!

2 sweet organic apples (e.g. Gala)	Suggested toppings:
maple syrup, to taste	Goji Nut Sprinkles (p37)
8 heaping TBSP non-dairy yogurt (160g)	Granola (p27)

1   Peel, core and dice the apples. Place in a bowl and use a hand blender to purée them until completely smooth. Taste test and add a little maple syrup, if needed.

2   In two ramekins, scoop 2 heaping TBSP yogurt, followed by half of the apple purée. Add another 2 heaping TBSP yogurt on top and smooth over to cover the apple. Sprinkle on the toppings and serve.

Mango Whip

Serves: 2   Hands on: 5 minutes   Ready in: 5 minutes

When frozen mango is blended, it has the most amazing silky smooth texture, making it perfect for home-made sorbets.

250g / 2 cups frozen mango chunks

120ml / ½ cup soya, rice or coconut drinking milk

1 TBSP maple syrup, or to taste

pinch of salt

1 If your house is warm, chill two ramekins or small bowls in the freezer for a few minutes.

2 - In a food processor: Whiz the mango chunks until broken down. Add the milk, syrup and salt, and continue blending until smooth. Stop now and then to scrape down the sides.

- Or in a power blender: Add the milk followed by the remaining ingredients. Use the tamper tool to push the mango onto the blade. Blend until smooth.

3 This dessert is best served immediately.

Alternative serving options:
- Swirl into coconut yogurt for a cooling summer dessert
- Blend with non-dairy milk to make a delicious 'ice cream' smoothie

Spiced Plum Compote

Serves: 4   Hands on: 10 minutes   Ready in: 25 minutes

This 'zingy' plum compote is one of my personal favourite desserts. And even though it's fruit, it's special enough to be considered a 'proper' dessert by the youngest member of our family. We love to layer it up with non-dairy yogurt to make a parfait or simply top it with a swirl of non-dairy cream and Goji Nut Sprinkles (p37).

500g / about 6-8 ripe, sweet plums
1 tsp zest from an unwaxed/organic orange
2½ TBSP freshly squeezed orange juice
½ tsp ground cinnamon

1 tsp vanilla extract
2 star anise
2½ TBSP coconut sugar or unrefined cane sugar

1   De-stone the plums and dice the flesh.

2   Add the plums and all the remaining ingredients to a small pan. Bring to the boil then reduce the heat to medium-low, cover with a lid, and simmer for 10 minutes.

3   Remove from the heat and leave to cool. As the plums cool, they will collapse into the liquid and turn it a beautiful rich colour. Remove the star anise. Taste test and add more sweetener, if needed.

4   For small children, blend smooth using a hand blender.

5   This compote will keep for five days in the refrigerator, or for months in the freezer.

Chocolate Orange Chia Pudding

Serves: 4   Hands on: 7 minutes   Ready in: 7 minutes

It's amazing how chia seeds transform into a silky-smooth pudding. What a yummy way to boost our omega-3 intake! And it's incredibly easy to make. It's simply a case of whizzing the ingredients together in a high speed blender. There's no end to the combination of ingredients and flavours you can add to the puddings. Chocolate orange is one of my family's favourites. The fresh zesty flavour of the orange works in harmony with the bitter dark chocolate to make one delicious dessert. It tastes decadent yet it's super healthy and packed with feel-good nutrients. It's also very filling so a little goes a long way. I find a ramekin or espresso cup is the perfect serving size.

80ml / ⅓ cup orange juice
300ml / 1¼ cups non-dairy milk
64g / 6 TBSP chia seeds
30g / 4 TBSP cacao or cocoa powder
4 soft pitted dates (e.g. Medjool)

½ tsp orange extract
1 TBSP maple syrup

Suggested garnish:
dark chocolate, finely chopped or grated
orange zest

1   Place the orange juice and milk in a blender, followed by the remaining ingredients. Give them a stir until they are coated in liquid. Blend on low speed until the dates are broken up, then move to high speed and continue blending until silky smooth. Stop now and then to scrape down the sides. Taste test and add a touch more orange extract or sweetener, if desired.

2   Pour into small ramekins or cups, sprinkle on the garnish and chill until ready to serve. It will keep for up to five days in the refrigerator.

Chocolate Banana Ice Cream

Serves: 3-4   Hands on: 5 minutes   Ready in: 5 minutes

One of my favourite ways to use over-ripe bananas is to transform them into ice cream. The bananas are frozen, then blended to make a dessert that's so creamy and delicious that it could easily pass as regular ice cream. This dessert is bound to be a great hit with all the family.

60ml / ¼ cup non-dairy milk
4 very ripe frozen peeled bananas
26g / 4 TBSP cacao or cocoa powder
1 tsp vanilla extract
1 TBSP maple syrup
2-3 TBSP almond butter, optional

Suggested toppings:
cacao nibs or dark choc chips
chopped mixed nuts (walnuts, toasted flaked almonds, pecans)

1   Slice the frozen bananas into coins.

2   Whiz the bananas in a food processor to break them up. Add the remaining ingredients and blend for a couple of minutes until smooth. Stop now and then to scrape down the sides and re-distribute the bananas around the bowl. For a while it may look like it's not going to blend smooth but be patient, it will!

3   Serve immediately as soft whip, or freeze in a wide shallow bowl for 2-4 hours for a scoopable ice cream. If left in the freezer for longer, the ice cream will freeze into a solid block. Leave at room temperature for 15 minutes, and it should be soft enough to scoop. Heating a metal scoop in a cup of boiling water will help to form smooth ice cream balls.

THE GOOD STUFF ♥
The natural sugars and fibre in bananas make them a good source of energy. They are also great stress busters! They contain nutrients that stimulate the production of serotonin, which has a calming and uplifting effect on the body and mind.

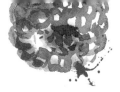

Summer Fruit 'Cheesecake'

Serves: 12   Hands on: 30 minutes   Ready in: 3 hours

When cashews are blended, they take on a beautiful creamy texture that makes them the perfect dairy substitute for cheesecakes. Filled with heart-healthy nuts and antioxidant-rich fruits, this dessert is one tasty, healthy (cholesterol-free!) alternative to regular cheesecake. It's far easier to make too – you simply blend the ingredients together. There's no baking involved!

Crust
150g / 1 cup almonds or pecans (or use a mix of the two)

180g / 1 cup soft, sticky dates (e.g. Medjool), pitted

1 tsp maple syrup

1 tsp vanilla extract

pinch of salt

Filling
280g / 2 cups raw cashews

160ml / ½ cup maple syrup

60ml / ¼ cup freshly squeezed lemon juice (about 2 lemons)

75g / ½ cup fresh raspberries

1 tsp vanilla extract

100g / ½ cup virgin coconut oil, melted

Topping
260g / 2 cups fresh or defrosted mixed summer fruit

1   First soften the cashews by soaking them in freshly boiled water for 30 minutes, then rinse and drain.

2   Grease the sides of a 23cm / 8 inch loose-bottomed tin with coconut oil and line the bottom with non-stick baking paper.

3   Place the almonds/pecans in a food processor and whiz into crumbs. Add the remaining crust ingredients and whiz until combined. Test the crumbs by pressing a small amount between your thumb and finger. If they stick together, they're ready. Tip them into the prepared tin and press down hard to form a crust.

4   Place the cashews in the food processor with the syrup, lemon juice, berries and vanilla extract. Process until the cashews are ground into a creamy mixture, stopping now and then to scrape down the bowl. Add the melted coconut oil and continue blending for a few minutes until the mixture is smooth. Taste test for smoothness. Check the sweetness levels and add a touch more syrup, if desired.

5   Tip the mixture on top of the crust and tap the tin on the worktop to remove any air bubbles. Smooth the surface with a knife. Freeze for about 2 hours until firm. Decorate with summer fruit before serving.

6   Stored in an airtight container, this dessert will keep for a couple of days in the refrigerator, or for two months in the freezer. If frozen, allow 30 minutes to an hour to thaw before serving.

THE GOOD STUFF ♥

Anthocyanins, which give berries their blue, red or purple hue, are powerful phytonutrients that act as antioxidants in the body, strengthening the immune system and protecting the body from disease. When buying berries (or any fruit or vegetable for that matter), always select the most vibrant ones. The more colourful they are, the more goodness they contain!

Pina Colada 'Cheesecake'

Serves: 12   Hands on: 30 minutes   Ready in: 3 hours

This dessert is bursting with the colours and flavours of my two favourite summer ingredients. If I can't be sitting on a Caribbean beach sipping Pina Coladas, then tucking into a slice of this scrumptious dessert is definitely the next best thing!

Crust

115g / ¾ cup almonds or pecans (or use a mix of the two)

50g / ½ cup desiccated coconut

180g / 1 cup soft, sticky dates (e.g. Medjool), pitted

1 tsp maple syrup

1 tsp vanilla extract

pinch of salt

Filling & topping

280g / 2 cups raw cashews

340g / 2 cups fresh sweet pineapple, cubed

80ml / ¼ cup maple syrup

6 drops rum essence, or to taste (or substitute with 1 tsp vanilla extract)

100g / ½ cup virgin coconut oil, melted

4-5 TBSP coconut chips

1   Soften the cashews by soaking them in freshly boiled water for 30 minutes, then rinse and drain.

2   Grease the sides of a 18-20cm (7-8 inch) loose-bottomed tin with coconut oil and line the bottom with non-stick baking paper.

3   Place the almonds/pecans in a food processor and blitz into crumbs. Add the remaining crust ingredients and whiz to combine. Test the crumbs by pressing a small amount between your thumb and finger. If they stick together, they're ready. Tip them into the prepared tin and press down firmly.

4   Pulse the pineapple in the food processor to crush it. Place in a sieve over a bowl and use the back of a spoon to press out as much juice from the pineapple as possible.

5   Place the cashews in the food processor and blitz into crumbs. Add the syrup, rum essence and 120ml / ½ cup pineapple juice from the drained pineapple. (If you don't have sufficient juice, top it up with water). Process for a few minutes until the cashews are ground into a creamy mixture, pausing now and then to scrape down the bowl. Add the melted coconut oil and continue processing until the mixture is completely smooth. Taste test for smoothness and sweetness. Add a touch more syrup, if desired.

6   Stir half of the crushed pineapple into the creamy cashew mixture.

7   Spoon the filling onto the crust and use a knife to smooth the top. Place in the freezer for about 2 hours, until it has firmed up. When ready to serve, top with the remaining crushed pineapple and a sprinkling of coconut chips.

8   Stored in an airtight container, this dessert will keep for a couple of days in the refrigerator or for two months in the freezer. If frozen, allow 30 minutes to an hour to thaw before serving.

Crunchy Nut Apple Crumble

Serves: 6   Hands on: 25 minutes   Ready in: 45 minutes

Apple Crumble is a quintessential British dessert. However, in contrast to the traditional recipe which is full of refined sugar and white flour, I've used nutrient-rich ingredients instead. The white flour is replaced with whole grain flour, oats and nuts which add great flavour, texture and lots of heart-healthy nutrients. By switching the traditional tart Bramleys for sweet apples, I've also been able to significantly reduce the amount of sugar needed. My family loves this 'Crunchy Nut Apple Crumble' and we hope you do too!

Apples

1kg / 7 medium-sized sweet apples (e.g. Gala)

60ml / 4 TBSP water

35g / 3 TBSP coconut sugar or unrefined cane sugar

1 tsp ground cinnamon

60g / ⅓ cup sultanas (or substitute with raisins)

Crumble

100g / ¾ cup wholemeal (whole wheat pastry) flour, chapatti flour or GF flour mix

1 tsp baking powder

½ tsp ground cinnamon

75g / ¾ cup rolled oats (quick oats, not jumbo)

50g / 4 TBSP coconut sugar or unrefined cane sugar

70g / 4½ TBSP dairy-free spread/vegan butter

30g / ¼ cup pecans, chopped

40g / ¼ cup almonds, chopped

½ - 1 TBSP Demerara (or turbinado) sugar

1   Preheat the oven to 190C (170C fan) / 375F.

2   Peel, core and slice the apples into bite-size pieces about 0.6cm / ¼ inch thick.

3   Place the water, sliced apples, sugar, cinnamon and sultanas in a large saucepan and stir through. Cover with a lid and cook on medium heat for 15 minutes, or until the apples have just started to soften but retain their shape. Give them a stir, now and then. Taste test and add a touch more sweetener, if needed.

4   Meanwhile, prepare the crumble: Place the flour, baking powder, cinnamon, oats and sugar in a mixing bowl. Rub the dairy-free spread/vegan butter into the mixture with your finger tips until it is fully incorporated. Stir in the nuts.

5   Spoon the apples into a 1.5 litre / 1½ quart ovenproof dish (about 22cm x 17cm x 6cm / 9" x 7" x 2½" in size). Level and lightly press down. Spoon the crumble evenly on top. Sprinkle on the Demerara sugar.

6   Bake for 20 minutes, or until the crumble is dry to the touch. Leave to rest for 5 minutes before serving.

7   This dessert is delicious served warm or cold, on its own or with natural non-dairy yogurt or custard. Stored in an airtight container, it will last five days in the refrigerator, or weeks in the freezer.

THE GOOD STUFF ♥
Apples are high in fibre, which helps
to balance blood sugar levels, aid
digestion and lower cholesterol
levels. Apple skin contains an
abundance of phytonutrients so
don't throw away the peel... eat it!

Old-Fashioned English Tea Loaf

Serves: 8-10   Hands on: 10 minutes   Ready in: 6 hours

It might be old-fashioned, but tea loaf rocks! It's perfect for serving for 'elevenses' or as a mid-afternoon 'pick me up'. It also makes a delicious lunchbox treat and after-school snack. As cakes go, this tea loaf is pretty healthy. It's filled with nutrient-rich dried fruits and whole grain flour, and it's fat free! It's also incredibly easy to make. You simply soak the dried fruit in a cup of tea for a few hours, then mix all the ingredients together and bake.

250ml / 1 cup strongly brewed black or green tea

225g / 1½ cups mixed dried fruit (e.g. raisins, sultanas, candied citrus peel)

110g / ½ cup unrefined cane sugar or coconut sugar

1 TBSP marmalade or apricot jam

227g / 1⅔ cups fine wholemeal (whole wheat pastry) flour or chapatti flour

2 tsp baking powder

1 tsp ground cinnamon or mixed spice

3 TBSP water

1   Soak the dried fruit in the brewed tea for 4-5 hours (or overnight).

2   Grease a 2lb loaf tin and line the bottom with non-stick baking paper (or use a non-stick loaf liner).

3   Preheat the oven to 160C (160C for fan also) / 325F.

4   Tip the dried fruit and any remaining tea into a mixing bowl. Stir in the sugar and marmalade/jam. Sift in the flour, baking powder and spice. Tip any remaining wheatgerm from the sieve into the bowl. Add 3 TBSP water and stir until thoroughly combined.

5   Tip the mixture into the prepared tin and level the top.

6   Bake for 1¼ hours, or until a skewer inserted in the middle comes out clean. Leave to rest in the tin for 30 minutes or so, then transfer to a wire rack until completely cooled.

7   Stored in an airtight container, the loaf will keep up to five days in the refrigerator. It also freezes well.

Bread Pudding

Serves: 16   Hands on: 20 minutes   Ready in: 2 hours

Bread pudding is one of my favourite childhood treats, but its name doesn't do it justice. It neither tastes like bread, nor is it a pudding. It's more like a sweet, fruity, dense cake. Bread pudding is traditionally made with cow's milk, butter and eggs but, despite being dairy-free, egg-free and lower in fat and sugar, this version is just as tasty. These days, a slice of bread pudding is often Lil' L's snack of choice for school and biking adventures. It's a delicious way to boost energy levels and will keep you feeling full up for hours. Be warned, it's very filling (so don't cut those squares too large!)

- 500g / 17½ oz wholemeal (whole wheat) bread
- 600ml / 2½ cups soya or almond milk
- 1 TBSP mixed spice
- ½ TBSP ground cinnamon
- 500g / 3½ cups mixed dried fruit (e.g. sultanas, raisins, candied citrus peel)

- zest of 1 unwaxed/organic lemon
- zest of 1 unwaxed/organic orange
- 50ml / ¼ cup organic rapeseed (canola) oil or other neutral-flavoured oil
- 100g / ½ cup unrefined cane sugar or coconut sugar
- 2 TBSP Demerara (or turbinado) sugar

1   Crumble the bread into a large mixing bowl. Pour in the milk and continue crumbling the bread until it has completely broken down. Stir in the mixed spice, cinnamon and dried fruits. Set aside for 30 minutes.

2   Preheat the oven to 180C (160C fan) / 350F. Grease and line a 20cm / 8 inch square baking tin with non-stick baking paper. Leave some paper overhanging the edges for easy removal.

3   Add the citrus zest, oil and sugar to the mixing bowl. Stir until thoroughly combined, then tip into the prepared tin. Press down and level with a silicone spatula. Sprinkle the Demerara sugar evenly on top. Bake for 1½ hours, or until a skewer inserted through the middle comes out clean. Leave to cool completely, then remove from the tin and slice.

4   Stored in an airtight container in the refrigerator, the bread pudding will keep for a week. It also freezes well.

Pecan Topped Banana Bread

Serves: 8-10   Hands on: 15 minutes   Ready in: 2 hours

Though I've given this loaf the traditional name of Banana Bread, it's so sweet and moist that it's definitely more cake-like than bread. I find it makes a lovely afternoon 'pick me up' with a cuppa. Kids love it too and it makes a great after-school treat.

3 over-ripe medium bananas, sliced

50ml / ¼ cup organic rapeseed (canola) oil or other neutral-flavoured oil

80g / ⅓ cup unrefined cane sugar or coconut sugar

1½ tsp vanilla extract

210g / 1½ cups fine wholemeal (whole wheat pastry) flour or chapatti flour

1½ tsp baking powder

½ tsp bicarbonate of soda (baking soda)

3 tsp ground cinnamon

¼ tsp salt

90g / ½ cup pitted dates, chopped

45g / ⅓ cup pecans, chopped

1   Preheat the oven to 180C (160C fan) / 350F. Grease and line a 2lb loaf tin with non-stick baking paper or use a non-stick loaf liner.

2   Place the sliced banana, oil, sugar and vanilla extract in a food processor and whiz until smooth (alternatively use a bowl and hand blender).

3   Sift the flour, baking powder, bicarbonate of soda, cinnamon and salt into a large mixing bowl. Tip any remaining wheatgerm from the sieve into the bowl. Stir to combine. Make a well in the middle and pour in the banana mixture. Gently stir until thoroughly combined. Stir in the dates. Tip the mixture into the prepared tin and level with the back of a spoon. Sprinkle the pecans on top and lightly press them into the batter.

4   Bake for 55 minutes, or until a skewer inserted through the middle comes out clean. Leave in the tin for at least 30 minutes, then transfer to a wire rack until completely cooled.

5   Stored in an airtight container, the loaf will keep for five days in the refrigerator. It also freezes well.

TIP For banana bread, you want to use over-ripe bananas – the blacker the better. So, if you've got some bananas languishing in the fruit bowl, this recipe is a great way to use them up.

THE GOOD STUFF ♥

Lemons are rich in vitamin C and antioxidant
phytonutrients such as flavonoids and
limonoids, which promote a strong immune
system. Vitamin C also boosts the body's
ability to absorb iron from food.

Lemon Drizzle Loaf

Serves: 8-10   Hands on: 15 minutes   Ready in: 2 hours

With its light fluffy texture, 'zingy' citrus flavour and flecks of bright yellow zest, this has got to be the perfect cake for spring. I first made this cake as a Mother's Day treat for my mum, and it fast became the most popular cake on my blog (and even featured in The Independent newspaper!) Since this is a special treat rather than 'every day' kind of cake, I haven't healthified it to the extreme. It is dairy-free and egg-free though, and contains far less fat and sugar than traditional lemon drizzle cakes, making it lighter in calories (and on our waistlines too!)

200g / ¾ cup + 3 TBSP unrefined cane sugar

40ml / 2 TBSP maple syrup

70ml / ⅓ cup organic rapeseed (canola) oil or other neutral-flavoured oil

240ml / 1 cup soya milk

2 tsp apple cider vinegar

30ml / 2 TBSP freshly squeezed lemon juice

zest of 2 unwaxed/organic lemons

250g / 1¾ cups plain (all purpose) flour

2 tsp baking powder

¼ tsp salt

Drizzle

2 TBSP freshly squeezed lemon juice

2 TBSP Demerara (or turbinado) sugar

1   Grease and line a 2lb loaf tin with non-stick baking paper (or use a non-stick loaf liner). Preheat the oven to 200C (180C fan) / 400F.

2   In a mixing bowl, whisk together the sugar, syrup, oil, milk, vinegar and lemon juice until fully combined. Stir in the lemon zest.

3   Sift one third of the dry ingredients (flour, baking powder, salt) into the bowl and whisk to combine. Repeat with the remaining two thirds, whisking each time.

4   Tip the mixture into the prepared tin. Place on the middle shelf in the oven and bake for 45 minutes, or until a skewer inserted into the middle comes out clean.

5   When the cake is baked, pierce all over with a skewer or toothpick. Whisk together the drizzle ingredients and distribute evenly over the top of the cake. Allow to cool in the tin for at least an hour (it will firm up as it cools), then transfer to a wire rack.

6   Once completely cooled, slice and serve or transfer to an airtight container. The cake will keep up to a week in the refrigerator, or for weeks in the freezer.

Orange & Almond Cake

Serves: 8-12   Hands on: 20 minutes   Ready in: 2 hours

Unlike regular cakes which are full of 'empty' calories, this cake is packed full of vitamins, minerals, antioxidants, protein and fibre. It also provides slow release energy thanks to the whole grain flour and almonds. It's the second most popular recipe on my blog (after the Lemon Drizzle) and has received great feedback. I would class this cake as a healthier 'eat any time' kind of cake, though some of my readers have served it at parties and told me that it went down a treat. It can easily be prepared in advance. In fact, we find it tastes even better a day or two after baking.

140g / 1 cup fine wholemeal (whole wheat pastry) flour or chapatti flour

140g / 1 cup plain (all purpose) flour

1½ tsp baking powder

½ tsp bicarbonate of soda (baking soda)

½ tsp salt

100g / 1 cup ground almonds (almond meal)

100ml / ½ cup organic rapeseed (canola) oil or other neutral-flavoured oil

150ml / ½ cup + 2 TBSP soya or almond milk

200ml / ⅔ cup maple syrup

½ TBSP zest from an unwaxed/ organic orange

60ml / ¼ cup freshly squeezed orange juice

1 tsp orange extract

½ tsp almond extract

Decorating options:
Orange Cashew Cream Frosting (p163) or apricot jam

3 TBSP toasted flaked almonds, crushed

1   Preheat the oven to 180C (160C fan) / 350F. Grease the sides of a 20cm / 8 inch loose-bottomed tin with oil and line the bottom with non-stick baking paper.

2   Sift the flours, baking powder, bicarbonate of soda and salt into a large bowl. Tip any remaining wheatgerm into the bowl. Add the ground almonds and stir through to combine.

3   In a separate bowl, use a fork to whisk together the oil, milk, syrup, orange zest, orange juice, orange extract and almond extract until fully combined.

4   Make a well in the dry ingredients, pour in the wet ingredients and stir to combine (but do not over mix). Pour the batter into the prepared tin.

5   Bake for 45 minutes, or until the cake is browned and feels springy when lightly pressed. Leave the cake in its tin until completely cooled (it will firm up as it cools).

6   Decorate with frosting or apricot jam and sprinkle toasted flaked almonds on top. Lightly press down on the almonds so that they stick. Chill in the refrigerator before serving.

7   Stored in an airtight container, this cake will last up to five days in the refrigerator. It also freezes well.

Orange Cashew Cream Frosting

Yield: about 240g / 3/4 cup frosting   Hands on: 10 minutes   Ready in: 70 minutes

In contrast to traditional frosting, this one is filled with nutrients including antioxidants, vitamins and minerals. It tastes delicious too! The cashews and coconut oil make it smooth and creamy, while the orange adds a zesty, fresh flavour. The quantities below will frost a 20cm / 8 inch cake, as seen in the picture overleaf.

110g / ¾ cup raw cashews
55ml / 3 TBSP maple syrup
½ TBSP zest from an unwaxed/ organic orange

30ml / 2 TBSP freshly squeezed orange juice
1 tsp orange extract
½ tsp vanilla extract
45g / 3 TBSP virgin coconut oil, melted

1   To soften the cashews, boil them in a pan of water for 15 minutes or soak in freshly boiled water for 30 minutes. Rinse in cold water and thoroughly drain.

2   Place the cashews in a food processor along with the syrup, zest, juice, orange extract and vanilla extract. Process until the cashews are ground into a creamy mixture. Stop now and then to scrape down the bowl. Add the melted coconut oil and continue blending for a few minutes until the mixture is completely smooth. Taste test for smoothness.

3   Scoop the frosting into a bowl and chill for one hour, or until firm enough to spread. The frosting will keep for five days in the refrigerator. It is also freezable.

Chocolate Celebration Cake

Serves: 12-16   Hands on: 20 minutes   Ready in: 2 hours

This is Lil' L's favourite birthday cake. He's requested it every birthday for the past six years! It's been a big hit with his friends too. The cake is perfect for serving at parties. It's easy to make and can be prepared in advance. In fact, we find it tastes even better a day or two after it's been made. There are many ways to dress this cake. My personal favourite is raspberry fruit spread for filling and a dusting of icing sugar on top. However, for birthday celebrations, nothing beats frosting and sprinkles.

480ml / 2 cups soya milk

2 tsp apple cider vinegar

200g / 1½ cups plain (all purpose) flour

200g / 1½ cups fine wholemeal (whole wheat pastry) flour or chapatti flour

60g / ½ cup cocoa powder

1 tsp baking powder

1 tsp bicarbonate of soda (baking soda)

½ tsp salt

140ml / ⅔ cup organic rapeseed (canola) oil or other neutral-flavoured oil

330g / 1⅔ cups unrefined cane sugar

2 tsp vanilla extract

Decorating options:

raspberry jam or fruit spread (e.g. St Dalfour) for filling and a dusting of icing (powdered) sugar on top

chocolate frosting (p166) and sprinkles

1   Preheat the oven to 180C (160C fan) / 350F. Grease the sides of two 23cm / 9 inch loose-bottomed tins and line the bottoms with non-stick baking paper.

2   In a large mixing bowl, whisk together the milk and vinegar, then set to one side.

3   In a separate large bowl, add the dry ingredients (flours, cocoa powder, baking powder, bicarbonate of soda and salt) and stir through to combine.

4   Add the oil, sugar and vanilla extract to the milk and vinegar, and whisk until fully combined. Sieve in a third of the dry ingredients and whisk to combine. Add another third and whisk to combine. Add the last third along with any remaining wheatgerm. Stir through to combine (but do not over stir).

5   Divide the batter equally between the prepared tins. Place on racks as close to the centre of the oven as possible. Bake for 40-50 minutes, until a skewer inserted into the middle comes out clean and the cakes are springy when lightly pressed. (In my oven I find the cake on the higher rack is ready after 40 minutes, and the cake on the lower rack sometimes needs an extra 5-10 minutes). If both cakes are domed, decide which one will be the bottom tier, cover with a clean tea cloth and gently press down to level.

6   Leave the cakes in their tins for at least an hour (they will firm up as they cool), then transfer to a wire rack. Once completely cooled, decorate the cakes and assemble. Chill before serving.

7   Stored in an airtight container, this cake will keep for up to a week in the refrigerator. It also freezes well. (See tips on p21).

Chocolate Sugar Frosting

Yield: about 250g / 3/4 cup   Hands on: 8 minutes   Ready in: 8 minutes

This recipe is for a dairy-free version of traditional sugar frosting. The quantities below are sufficient for frosting the centre and top of a 23cm / 9 inch cake.

150g / 1 cup icing (powdered) sugar
35g / ¼ cup cocoa powder

50g / 4 TBSP dairy-free spread/vegan butter
1-1½ TBSP water

1   Sieve the icing sugar and cocoa powder into a large bowl. Add the dairy-free spread/butter and 1 TBSP water. Stir with a metal spoon until it starts to combine, then beat with electric beaters until light and fluffy. If the frosting looks a little stiff, add another ½ TBSP water and keep beating. This frosting will keep for a week in the refrigerator. It's also freezable.

Chocolate Cashew Cream Frosting

Yield: about 275g / 1 cup   Hands on: 10 minutes   Ready in: 40 minutes

Made with a blend of creamy cashews, virgin coconut oil and maple syrup, this frosting is far healthier than traditional frosting. It tastes far nicer too (in my opinion!) The quantities below are sufficient for frosting the centre and top of a 23cm / 9 inch cake.

130g / 1 cup raw cashews
30g / 4 TBSP cocoa powder
15ml / 1 TBSP non-dairy milk
60ml / 3 TBSP maple syrup

1 tsp vanilla extract
45g / 3 TBSP virgin coconut oil, melted
pinch of salt

1   First, soften the cashews by boiling them in a pan of water for 15 minutes or soaking in freshly boiled water for 30 minutes. Rinse in cold water and thoroughly drain.

2   Place the cashews, cocoa powder, milk, syrup and vanilla extract in a food processor and whiz until the cashews are broken down into a creamy mixture. Stop now and then to scrape down the bowl. Add the melted coconut oil and salt, and continue processing until the mixture is completely smooth. Taste test for smoothness and flavour. Add a touch more cocoa, sweetener or vanilla extract, if desired.

3   The frosting will thicken when chilled, so if it looks too thick to spread at this stage, add ½ TBSP milk at a time and continue processing until you reach a spreadable consistency. Scoop into a bowl and chill until required. This frosting will keep for a week in the refrigerator. It's also freezable.

Double Chocolate Cranberry Oatmeal Cookies

Makes: 12   Hands on: 20 minutes   Ready in: 35 minutes

Set against a backdrop of dark chocolate, the cranberries glisten like ruby gems. While they taste decadent, these cookies contain lots of good stuff. The whole grain flour and oats provide protein, fibre and slow release energy, while the cocoa and cranberries add antioxidants, vitamins and minerals.

45ml / 3 TBSP soya or almond milk

35ml / 3 TBSP organic rapeseed (canola) oil or other neutral-flavoured oil

1 tsp vanilla extract

80g / heaping ⅓ cup unrefined cane sugar

70g / ½ cup fine wholemeal (whole wheat pastry) flour or chapatti flour

20g / 3 TBSP cocoa powder

¼ tsp baking powder

¼ tsp bicarbonate of soda (baking soda)

¼ tsp salt

50g / ½ cup rolled oats (quick oats, not jumbo)

50g / ⅓ cup dried cranberries (preferably sweetened with fruit juice)

25g / 2 TBSP dark choc chips

1   Preheat the oven to 180C (160C fan) / 350F. Line a large baking sheet with non-stick baking paper.

2   Place the milk, oil, vanilla extract and sugar in a mixing bowl and whisk with a fork until fully combined.

3   In a separate bowl, combine the flour, cocoa powder, baking powder, bicarbonate of soda, salt and oats. Add these ingredients to the wet ingredient bowl and stir to combine. Stir in the cranberries and choc chips.

4   Scoop slightly heaped tablespoons of dough onto the prepared baking sheet. With damp fingers, press the dough into cookie shapes (these cookies don't spread much).

5   Bake for 12 minutes, or until the cookies are dry to the touch. Leave the cookies on the tray for a few minutes (they will firm up as they cool), then loosen from the baking paper using a thin spatula/slotted turner and transfer to a wire rack.

6   Once completely cooled, store in an airtight container where they will keep for a couple of weeks. These cookies also freeze well.

Spiced Orange Oatmeal Raisin Cookies

Makes: 9   Hands on: 20 minutes   Ready in: 35 minutes

Filled with warming spices and zesty orange, these cookies make a lovely autumn treat, though I'll happily eat them all year round! Not only do they taste delicious, but they smell wonderful too. As they bake, the kitchen is filled with the most beautiful spicy orange aroma. Packed with whole grains and dried fruits, these cookies are great little energy boosters.

30ml / 2 TBSP soya or almond milk

40ml / 3 TBSP organic rapeseed (canola) oil or other neutral-flavoured oil

40g / ¼ cup unrefined cane sugar or coconut sugar

1 tsp orange extract

½ tsp vanilla extract

½ TBSP zest from 1 organic/unwaxed orange

70g / ¾ cup rolled oats (quick oats, not jumbo)

50g / ⅓ cup fine wholemeal (whole wheat pastry) flour or chapatti flour

½ tsp ground cinnamon

¼ tsp ground ginger

pinch of ground nutmeg

¼ tsp bicarbonate of soda (baking soda)

¼ tsp baking powder

¼ tsp salt

45g / ¼ cup raisins

1   Preheat the oven to 180C (160C fan) / 350F. Line a large baking sheet with non-stick baking paper.

2   Add the milk, oil and sugar to a mixing bowl and whisk together with a fork until fully combined. Whisk in the orange extract, vanilla extract and orange zest.

3   In a separate bowl, mix together the dry ingredients (oats, flour, spices, bicarbonate of soda, baking powder and salt). Tip the dry ingredients into the wet ingredient bowl and stir to combine. Stir in the raisins.

4   Scoop rounded tablespoons of dough onto the prepared baking sheet. Using damp hands, press the dough balls into cookie shapes (these cookies don't spread much).

5   Bake for 12 minutes, or until lightly browned and dry to the touch.

6   Leave to cool for a few minutes (the cookies will firm up as they cool), then use a thin spatula/slotted turner to slide them off the baking paper and transfer to a wire rack.

7   Once completely cooled, store in an airtight container, where they will keep for a week. They also freeze really well.

Gingerbread Cookies

Makes: 12   Hands on: 15 minutes   Ready in: 35 minutes

Freshly baked, these cookies are crisp on the outside with a soft, chewy centre. Molasses adds a wonderful depth of flavour and colour to the cookies. It also boosts their nutrient content. While white sugar has no nutritional value whatsoever, the molasses that gets left behind in the sugar-refining process is literally brimming with nutrients. It's rich in vitamin B6 and a host of minerals including calcium, iron, magnesium, potassium, manganese and selenium. Traditionally, this by-product of the sugar-refining industry has been used to feed livestock, while humans consume the empty calorie, unhealthy white sugar. Crazy eh?

70g / ⅓ cup unrefined cane sugar or coconut sugar

50ml / ¼ cup organic rapeseed (canola) oil or other neutral-flavoured oil

65g / 3 TBSP black treacle (molasses) or Blackstrap molasses

22g / 1½ TBSP soya or almond milk

½ tsp vanilla extract

120g / ¾ cup & 2 TBSP fine wholemeal (whole wheat pastry) flour or chapatti flour

1 – 1½ tsp ground ginger

½ tsp ground cinnamon

pinch of ground nutmeg

¼ tsp baking powder

¼ tsp bicarbonate of soda (baking soda)

¼ tsp salt

1   Preheat the oven to 200C (180C fan) / 400F. Line two baking sheets with non-stick baking paper.

2   Place the sugar, oil, molasses, milk and vanilla extract in a mixing bowl and whisk with a fork until smooth and fully combined.

3   Place the flour, spices, baking powder, bicarbonate of soda and salt in a separate bowl and stir through. Tip half the dry ingredients into the wet ingredient bowl and stir to combine. Add the remaining dry ingredients and keep stirring until the mixture comes together in a firm dough.

4   Scoop slightly rounded tablespoons of dough and arrange six on each baking sheet. With damp fingers, press the dough into a thin cookie shape.

5   Bake in the centre of the oven for 9 minutes, or until dry to the touch. (The cookies will still feel soft, but they firm up as they cool).

6   Leave the cookies on the baking sheets until they are firm, then use a thin spatula/slotted turner to remove them from the baking paper and transfer to a wire rack.

7   When completely cool, store in an airtight container where they will keep for a couple of weeks. They also freeze well. Leave at room temperature for about 10 minutes before serving.

THE GOOD STUFF ♥

Ginger has been valued for its aromatic, culinary and medicinal
properties for thousands of years. It contains potent
anti-inflammatory compounds called gingerols, which help to
relieve swelling and improve circulation. Ginger also soothes
the digestive system and can help relieve migraine headaches.

Dark Chocolate Florentines
with Cranberry & Orange

Makes: 12   Hands on: 20 minutes   Ready in: 40 minutes

I'd been dreaming about Florentines ever since I'd caught sight of them in the patisserie shops of Venice. They looked so decadent with their glistening tops and dark chocolate bottoms. Back home, I couldn't wait to try my hand at creating my own dairy-free version.

Florentines are typically made with cane sugar, honey, butter, candied cherries, candied citrus peel and almonds, but I ended up subbing five of the six ingredients. Only the almonds stayed! While I can't claim that these Florentines are authentic, they are truly scrumptious. They're crisp on the outside, chewy in the centre with a melt-in-your-mouth chocolate bottom. And since each Florentine only contains one teaspoon of mixture, in my eyes, that makes it totally acceptable to go back for a second or third. I also love to give them as gifts, stacked in a cellophane bag and tied with a ribbon.

30g / ¼ cup toasted flaked almonds

30g / 2 TBSP dairy-free spread/vegan butter or aroma-free coconut butter

30g / 3 TBSP coconut sugar or unrefined cane sugar

30ml / 2 TBSP maple syrup

18g / 2 TBSP fine wholemeal (whole wheat pastry) flour, chapatti flour or GF flour mix

30g / 3 TBSP dried cranberries (preferably sweetened with fruit juice), finely chopped

zest of 1 unwaxed/organic orange

100g / 3½ oz dark chocolate, chopped into small pieces (or use dark choc chips)

1   Preheat the oven to 180C (160C fan) / 350F. Line two large baking sheets with non-stick baking paper.

2   Crush the almonds between your fingers to break them up.

3   In a small pan, gently heat the dairy-free spread/butter. Once it has melted, whisk in the sugar and syrup. Remove from the heat and whisk in the flour. Stir in the almonds, cranberries and zest. You want to get the mixture as uniform as possible so that the Florentines spread evenly as they bake.

4   Drop six rounded teaspoons of mixture onto one baking sheet. Be sure to space them out to give them plenty of room to spread. Add another six teaspoons to the second baking sheet. Using damp fingers, press down on the Florentines to flatten slightly and shape into circles.

5   Bake in the preheated oven for 8 minutes, or until the edges of the Florentines have browned. Leave to cool. (They will be very soft when they come out of the oven, but they firm up as they cool).

6   Place the chocolate in a heat-proof bowl set over a pan of gently simmering water (make sure the water doesn't touch the bowl). When the chocolate has melted, remove from the heat. If the chocolate's very runny, stir until it thickens slightly. Using a knife, coat the bottom of each Florentine. Before the chocolate sets, wiggle a fork across it to form a wavy pattern.

7   Chill the Florentines until fully set, then transfer to an airtight container. Stored in the refrigerator, they will keep for at least a couple of weeks. They also freeze really well.

TIP   For this recipe, I recommend weighing the ingredients using scales as it's more precise than measuring with tablespoons. The shape and 'laciness' of the Florentines will vary depending on the size of the fruit and nut pieces, and the type of flour and fat used. However, whatever their shape, I guarantee they will be delicious!

Giant Peanut Butter Cups

Makes: 6-8 large cups   Hands on: 30 minutes   Ready in: 60 minutes

These treats are so simple to make but definitely have the 'wow' factor. They're giant in size so perfect for sharing with your loved ones. As a Valentine's treat, I love to shape them into giant hearts using a silicone heart cake mould. For a more traditional peanut butter cup, round silicone cake moulds or paper cases can be used. If you use paper cases, I recommend doubling them up to make them extra sturdy. Almond butter makes a delicious substitute for anyone with a peanut allergy.

200g / 7 oz 70% dark chocolate, chopped into small pieces

1 TBSP virgin coconut oil, divided (optional)

70g / ¼ cup smooth natural peanut butter (or substitute with almond butter)

20g / 2 TBSP icing (powdered) sugar or ground coconut sugar

½ tsp vanilla extract

¼ tsp sea salt

1   Place half of the chocolate (and optional ½ TBSP coconut oil) in a heat-proof bowl set over a pan of gently simmering water (make sure the water doesn't touch the bowl). When the chocolate has fully melted, remove from the heat.

2   Spoon about 2 tsp melted chocolate into each mould. Tilt the moulds so that the chocolate coats the sides to a height of about 1cm / just under ½ inch. (You may not use all the melted chocolate, but that's fine. Just leave it in the bowl).

3   Pop the moulds in the refrigerator until the chocolate is solid.

4   In a small bowl, mix together the peanut butter, sugar, vanilla extract and sea salt. (If using coconut sugar, first grind it into a fine powder using an electric grinder). Taste test and add more sweetener or salt if desired.

5   Add the remaining half of the chocolate pieces (and optional ½ TBSP coconut oil) to the heat-proof bowl over the pan of water. Gently heat until the chocolate melts.

6   When the chocolate base is set, spoon a small amount of peanut butter filling into the centre of each mould (I use 1-1½ tsp per mould). Use the back of a teaspoon to level the filling, but leave a gap round all sides. Spoon melted chocolate on top and tilt the mould to fill in the sides.

7   If you have any chocolate left over, pour it onto a piece of baking paper to create a chocolate 'puddle'. You can keep this in the refrigerator for another recipe. Any leftover peanut butter is delicious spread on toast or apple slices.

8   Chill the peanut butter cups until completely solid. Stored in an airtight container, these treats will keep for weeks. If your house is warm, store them in the refrigerator or freezer.

TIP   The addition of coconut oil makes the chocolate slightly softer and creamier. Without the oil, the chocolate has a 'snap' to it. I love it both ways!

Coconut Chocolate Bark
with Goji Berries & Pecans

Makes: 20   Hands on: 20 minutes   Ready in: 1 hour

If you haven't made your own chocolate before, you must give this recipe a try. It couldn't be easier! The chocolate is made using virgin coconut oil instead of cocoa butter, which gives it a silky smooth 'melt in your mouth' texture. The recipe below features one of my all-time favourite fruit and nut combinations - pecans and goji berries - but feel free to use your own.

65g / ⅓ cup virgin coconut oil

50g / ½ cup cacao or cocoa powder

2-3 TBSP Sweet Freedom fruit syrup or maple syrup

2½ TBSP goji berries, divided

60g / ½ cup pecans, raw or toasted

1   Line a loaf tin (or other container about 20cm x 9cm / 8" x 3½" in size) with non-stick baking paper. Leave sufficient hanging over the edges so you can lift it out.

2   Roughly chop the pecans and place 2 TBSP in a mini food processor along with 2 TBSP goji berries (I use the bowl attachment that came with my hand blender). Pulse until finely chopped.

3   Place the coconut oil in a heat-proof bowl set over a pan of gently simmering water (make sure the water doesn't touch the bowl). When the oil has melted, whisk in the cacao/cocoa powder and syrup. Taste test, and add more sweetener, if needed.

4   Stir in the finely chopped pecans and goji berries, along with another 2-3 TBSP of the chopped pecans.

5   Lift the bowl off the saucepan and dry the bottom with a tea cloth (this will prevent any water dripping into the chocolate and ruining it).

6   Pour the chocolate into the prepared container. Tap the container on the worktop to remove any air bubbles. Sprinkle the remaining pecans and goji berries on top. Lightly press them into the chocolate.

7   Place in the freezer until fully set (around 1 hour). Once set, lift the chocolate out of the container and cut into pieces using a sharp, smooth-edged knife.

8   Coconut oil becomes soft at room temperature, so the chocolate is best served straight from the refrigerator or freezer. In an airtight container, the chocolate will keep for weeks.

THE GOOD STUFF ♥
Goji berries (aka wolfberries, lycium berries)
are packed with antioxidant phytonutrients
including flavonoids, polyphenols and carotenoids.
They are also a good source of trace minerals
iron, copper and selenium.

Dark Chocolate Cranberry Truffles

Makes: 20   Hands on: 30 minutes   Ready in: 1 hour 20 minutes

Chocolate coated with a fudgy centre speckled with shiny red cranberries, these truffles are the perfect treat for the festive season. On Christmas Eve, we love to package them in chocolate boxes and give them to our neighbours and friends. Packed full of nutrient-rich, feel-good ingredients, this is one festive treat that you definitely won't regret indulging in.

30g / ¼ cup walnuts or pecans

35g / ¼ cup raw cashews

110g / ½ cup soft, sticky dates (e.g. Medjool), pitted

20g / 3 TBSP cacao or cocoa powder

1½ tsp vanilla extract

1 tsp maple syrup

pinch of salt

35g / 4 TBSP dried cranberries (preferably sweetened with fruit juice)

100g / 3½ oz dark chocolate, chopped into small pieces (or use dark choc chips)

1   Whiz the nuts in a food processor to break them down. Add the dates, cacao/cocoa powder, vanilla extract, maple syrup and salt. Process until the mixture has formed crumbs that easily stick together when pressed between your thumb and forefinger. Add the cranberries and process until they are roughly chopped. Taste test and add a touch more cocoa or sweetener, if desired.

2   Line a tray with non-stick baking paper. Scoop ½ TBSP mixture and roll it into a ball, then place on the paper. Repeat with the remaining mixture.

3   Place the chocolate in a heat-proof bowl set over a pan of gently simmering water (make sure the water doesn't touch the bowl). When the chocolate has melted, switch off the heat.

4   Using a metal spoon, quickly roll each truffle in the chocolate. Place the truffle on a fork and gently shake off the excess chocolate. Place the truffle back on the lined tray. Repeat with the remaining truffles. Chill in the refrigerator until set.

5   If you have any melted chocolate left over, pour it onto a piece of baking paper to form a chocolate 'puddle' then chill until set. You can save this for another recipe.

6   Stored in an airtight container, these truffles will keep for weeks in the refrigerator or freezer.

Lemon Coconut Energy Bites

Makes: 12   Hands on: 15 minutes   Ready in: 15 minutes

These energy bites are packed with ingredients that help to boost and sustain energy levels, making them a great mid-morning or afternoon 'pick me up'. Compact and easy to transport, they're my number one snack for road trips and hiking/biking adventures. They can be flavoured in a variety of ways and the texture adapted to make them smooth or crunchy. One of our all-time favourites is this tropical-tasting lemon and coconut bite.

22g / ¼ cup desiccated coconut

1 TBSP coconut sugar

50g / ½ cup rolled oats (quick oats, not jumbo)

40g / ¼ cup raw cashews

35g / ¼ cup walnuts

120g / ½ cup soft, sticky dates (e.g. Medjool), pitted

½ – 1 tsp zest from an unwaxed/ organic lemon

2 TBSP freshly squeezed lemon juice

1 tsp maple syrup

pinch of salt

1   Mix together the desiccated coconut and sugar in a shallow container.

2   Place the oats, cashews and walnuts in a food processor and whiz into fine crumbs. Add the dates, lemon zest, lemon juice, maple syrup and salt. Process until the mixture comes together in a ball. Taste test and add a touch more lemon zest or sweetener, if desired.

3   Scoop level tablespoons of the mixture. Roll into balls, then roll in the coconut sugar mixture. Repeat until all the dough is used. Chill in the refrigerator before serving (they will firm up as they chill).

4   Stored in an airtight container, these energy bites will keep for a week in the refrigerator, or for weeks in the freezer.

Cocoa Lime Energy Bites

Makes: 12   Hands on: 15 minutes   Ready in: 15 minutes

As we head into spring, I start to crave lighter foods and fresh citrus flavours. For me, these Cocoa Lime Energy Bites are spot on for this time of year. They're chocolatey but not too rich, they're fresh and zesty thanks to the lime, and they're lighter than classic energy bites as I've substituted some of the nuts for grains. I also like to add a handful of cacao nibs for a delicious chocolatey 'crunch', as well as more of those amazing raw cocoa nutrients.

- 22g / ¼ cup desiccated coconut
- 1 TBSP coconut sugar
- 50g / ½ cup rolled oats (quick oats, not jumbo)
- 40g / ¼ cup raw cashews
- 35g / ¼ cup walnuts
- 1 TBSP shelled hemp seeds, optional
- 2 TBSP cacao or cocoa powder

- 120g / ½ cup soft, sticky dates (e.g. Medjool), pitted
- ½ – 1 tsp zest from an unwaxed/organic lime
- 2 TBSP freshly squeezed lime juice
- 1 tsp maple syrup
- pinch of salt
- 2 TBSP cacao nibs, optional

1   Mix together the desiccated coconut and sugar in a shallow container.

2   Place the oats, cashews, walnuts and hemp seeds in a food processor and whiz into crumbs. Add the cacao/cocoa powder, dates, lime zest, lime juice, maple syrup and salt. Process until the dates are broken down. Add the cacao nibs, and continue processing until the mixture comes together in a ball. Taste test and add a touch more cacao/cocoa, lime zest or sweetener, if desired.

3   Scoop level tablespoons of the mixture. Roll into balls, then roll in the coconut sugar mixture. Repeat until all the dough is used. Chill in the refrigerator. As they chill, they will firm up.

4   Stored in an airtight container, these energy bites will keep for a week in the refrigerator, or for weeks in the freezer.

Tamari Roasted Almonds & Sunflower Seeds

Yield: about 150g / 1 cup   Hands on: 2 minutes   Ready in: 12 minutes

Hugely popular with Lil' L and his friends, these roasted nuts and seeds make a tasty savoury snack. Be sure to roast a large batch as they'll be gone in no time at all!

110g / ¾ cup almonds
40g / ¼ cup sunflower seeds

½ TBSP tamari or reduced-salt soy sauce
olive oil, for greasing

1   Preheat the oven to 180C (160C fan) / 350F. Line a baking tray with non-stick baking paper and lightly spray or brush with oil.

2   Place the nuts and seeds in a bowl. Sprinkle on the soy sauce and stir until fully coated.

3   Tip onto the prepared tray and roast for 10 minutes. Give them a stir halfway through the cooking time. The almonds are ready when they smell fragrant and are lightly browned on the inside.

4   Leave to cool before serving. (As they cool, they will become crunchy). Store in an airtight container in the refrigerator or a cool pantry, where they will keep for weeks.

Maple Glazed Nuts

Yield: about 300g / 2 cups   Hands on: 5 minutes   Ready in: 8 minutes

Packed full of nutty goodness, this tasty treat is so easy and quick to prepare. If, like us, you're tempted to devour the lot in one go, try bagging the nuts in individual-size portions and hide them in the refrigerator or freezer.

110g / 1 cup pecans
160g / 1 cup roasted or blanched almonds

80ml / 4 TBSP maple syrup

1   Preheat a large frying pan (skillet) on medium-high heat. Add the nuts and dry fry for 2 minutes, stirring continuously. Add the maple syrup and continue stirring until the syrup has caramelised and become very sticky (about 3 minutes).

2   Using a spatula, space out the nuts on a large piece of non-stick baking paper. As they cool, the nuts will firm up and become shiny. Once completely cooled, store in an airtight container in the refrigerator or freezer, where they will keep for weeks (but I'm sure they'll be gone long before then!)

Rosemary Roasted Cashews

Yield: about 145g / 1 cup   Hands on: 5 minutes   Ready in: 15 minutes

Wrapped in cellophane bags, these nuts make a lovely addition to festive hampers or Christmas stockings. Be warned, they are very addictive!

140g / 1 cup raw cashews
1 tsp extra virgin olive oil
1 tsp maple syrup

1 TBSP dried rosemary
sea salt or pink Himalayan salt

1   Preheat the oven to 180C (160C fan) / 350F. Line a baking tray with non-stick baking paper.

2   Place the cashews in a bowl. Drizzle in the oil and syrup, and stir until the cashews are fully coated. Sprinkle in the rosemary and stir through.

3   Tip the cashews onto the prepared tray. Scrape any remaining rosemary out of the bowl and transfer it to the tray. Add a light sprinkling of salt. Place on the centre rack of the oven and bake for 5 minutes. Give the cashews a stir so that they brown evenly, then bake for another 5 minutes or until golden. Keep an eye on the nuts towards the end of the cooking time to ensure they don't burn.

4   Remove from the oven. Add another light sprinkle of salt, then leave the cashews to cool completely (they will crisp up as they cool). Transfer to an airtight jar. Scrape off any remaining rosemary from the baking tray and add it to the jar. The cashews are best stored in the refrigerator where they will keep for weeks.

Sweet 'n' Salty Crispy Kale

Serves: 2-3   Hands on: 6 minutes   Ready in: 20 minutes

If you like the crispy seaweed served in Chinese restaurants, I'm pretty confident you'll love crispy kale. It's proven to be a great way to encourage Lil' L to eat big handfuls of this leafy green vegetable. I often put a bowl out as a starter, side dish or snack, and it's demolished in no time at all. We love to flavour our crispy kale 'sweet 'n' salty', but feel free to experiment with your favourite spice mixes.

2 large handfuls of curly kale, thick stalks removed (about 100g)

½ - 1 TBSP coconut sugar or unrefined cane sugar

¼ tsp salt

½ TBSP olive oil

3 TBSP Gomasio (p185) or sesame seeds

1   Preheat the oven to 150C (130C fan) / 300F. Line two large baking sheets with non-stick baking paper.

2   Wash the kale and tear into large bite-size pieces (the kale will shrink as it cooks). Use a salad spinner to dry the kale. Place the kale in a bowl and give it a final dab with kitchen paper. Sprinkle in the sugar, salt, oil and sesame seasoning. Massage the kale with your hands until it is fully coated in oil.

3   Spread out the kale on the prepared baking sheets. Make sure that none of the leaves overlap or are folded over, otherwise they will steam (rather than roast) and won't crisp up. Depending on the amount of kale you have and the size of your baking sheets, you may need to cook the kale in two batches.

4   Place the kale in the oven and cook for 14 minutes. Check the leaves. If they are not 100% crispy, continue cooking and check at 2 minute intervals.

5   Crispy kale is most delicious eaten warm, straight from the oven. However, once completely cooled, it can be stored in an airtight container where it will keep for up to a week.

THE GOOD STUFF ♥
Kale has powerful anti-inflammatory, detoxifying and cholesterol-lowering properties. It is one of the most nutrient-dense foods available. Just one cup of cooked kale provides 354% of the vitamin A RDA, 89% of vitamin C and 1328% of vitamin K. It is also a good source of calcium, dietary fibre and omega 3.

Gomasio Seasoning

Yield: about 80g / 3/4 cup   Hands on: 5 minutes   Ready in: 10 minutes

Gomasio is a Japanese condiment made with toasted sesame seeds and salt. It makes a wonderful seasoning for stir fry dishes as well as crispy kale.

80g / ½ cup sesame seeds   ¼ tsp salt

1   Toast the sesame seeds in a dry frying pan (skillet) on medium heat, stirring continuously until they start to turn golden and fragrant. Tip onto a plate and leave to cool. Roughly grind the sesame and salt with a mortar and pestle or an electric coffee/spice grinder. If using an electric grinder, you will only need a couple of quick blasts (too much grinding and you'll end up with sesame butter!)

2   Store the gomasio in an airtight container in the refrigerator, where it will keep for weeks.

Acknowledgements

Thank you Mark and Lucien for being my rocks of support and such enthusiastic taste testers. I'm amazed that, after all these years, you still haven't grown tired of these recipes and my endless attempts to tweak them to perfection.

Thank you to my friends and family for your unshakeable enthusiasm for the project and for spurring me on when the summit of the mountain seemed such a long way off. I can't quite believe I've made it! A special shout out goes to those who have patiently put up with my incessant chattering about the book these past five years including Nicky Dye, Cheryl Nield de Crespo, Sira Franco, Esther Sanchez, Helen Begum, Naomi Grady, Joni and the Ashpole family, Kelsang Virya, Lucy at North, Phil Johnston, Mike Kielkowski, Coral Collins, Dan & Paula Knowlson, Isabella Mori and my youngest supporters - Florrie and Winnie Priday. A special thank you goes to Janet Fernihough. I hope it makes you smile when you see the photos as every single one was shot using your trusty tripod.

A big thank you to my international team of recipe testers, including Mary Doak, Anne-Marie van Benthum, Katja Haudenhuyse, Rachel Jacobs, Sue Merritt, Jacqui Edwards, Gae Matthews, Gary Wilson-Garner, Becky Maybury, Patricia Owens, Hannah Short, Vicky Rockcliffe, Amanda Serif, Laura Seymour, Susan Rush, Bo Novak, Ema at De Tout Coeur Limousin, Jen Farrant, Victoria Wells, Sarah Johnson, Jess Milton, Gina Grainger-Windridge, Sue Denby, Justine Butler, Sandy Sparrow, Judith Kelly, Caroline Cooper, Bettina Schelkle, Ceilidh Jackson-Baker, Mary Saylor, Christopher Penny, Valeria Rinaldi, 'JP' Petrides and Hiranya de Alwis Jayasinghe. You made the recipe testing phase so smooth and easy. Thanks to you, the recipes are more accessible and foolproof than ever.

Thank you Professor C Thomas Campbell, Dr Michael Greger, Dr Joel Furhman, Dr Cadwell Esseltyn, Dr Dean Ornish, Dr Neil Barnard, Dr John McDougall, Dr Garth Davis, Dr Joel Kahn and all the other doctors and researchers that have worked tirelessly to raise the profile of whole-food plant-based diets and show how they can help people live disease-free, healthy, happy lives. My family are reaping the benefits of your work.

Thank you to Juliet Gellatley and the team at Viva!, Fiona Oakes at the Tower Hill Stables Animal Sanctuary and every other campaigner that has devoted their life to raising awareness of how we can live compassionate, cruelty-free lives. I hope that in my own small way through this book and my blog, I'm able to help spread the message and show just how easy it is to eat plant-based and avoid animal exploitation.

I would like to thank all the Bit of the Good Stuff blog readers. I appreciate every interaction we have whether that be via the blog, email or social media. I feel incredibly fortunate to be a part of such a friendly, supportive and dynamic blogging community, and I'm especially grateful to fellow bloggers and authors Aimee Ryan and Ellie Bedford for all the advice and encouragement they've given me for the production of this book.

And finally, a huge, special thank you to Catriona Archer for working her magic and transforming my words and images into this beautiful book. I'll never forget all those hours we spent together in summer 2016 and your tireless enthusiasm and passion for the project. Thanks to you, this book truly has been a labour of love from start to finish.

References

1 Physicians Committee for Responsible Medicine. *Vegetarian Diets: Advantages for Children* (available to download at http://www.pcrm.org); Joel Furhman, M.D. 2005. *Disease-Proof Your Child*. New York: St Martin's Griffin; Michael Greger, MD with Gene Stone. 2016. *How Not To Die*. London: Macmillan

2 Food and Agriculture Organization (FAO) of the United Nations. 2006. *Livestock's Long Shadow* (available to download at http://www.fao.org)

3 World Health Organization (WHO). *Recommendations for preventing osteoporosis* (available to view at http://www.who.int); Report of a joint FAO/WHO expert consultation. 2001. *Human Vitamin and Mineral Requirements. Chapter 11. Calcium* (available to view at http://www.fao.org)

4 T. Colin Campbell, PhD & Thomas M. Campbell II, MD. 2006. *The China Study*. Dallas: BenBella Books. p204-211

5 Michael Greger, MD with Gene Stone. 2016. *How Not To Die*. London: Macmillan. p329

The nutrition data in 'The Good Stuff' tips is sourced from NutritionData.com

Resources

While by no means exhaustive, in this section I've listed some of the books, documentaries and websites that I have personally found informative and inspiring.

Books
Disease-Proof Your Child (2005), Joel Fuhrman, M.D.
Eating Animals (2009), Jonathan Safran Foer
Finding Ultra (2012), Rich Roll
How Not To Die (2015), Michael Greger, M.D. with Gene Stone
No Meat Athlete (2013), Matt Frazier
Super Immunity (2011), Joel Fuhrman, M.D.
The China Study (2006), T. Colin Campbell, PhD & Thomas M. Campbell II, MD
The Eat to Live Diet (2003), Dr Joel Fuhrman
The Food Revolution (2011), John Robbins

Documentaries
A Delicate Balance (http://www.adelicatebalance.com.au)
Cowspiracy: The Sustainability Secret (http://www.cowspiracy.com)
Forks over Knives (http://www.forksoverknives.com/the-film/)
Vegucated (http://www.getvegucated.com)

Websites
NutritionFacts.org (http://nutritionfacts.org)
Physicians Committee for Responsible Medicine (http://www.pcrm.org/health)
The Vegan Society (https://www.vegansociety.com)
The Vegetarian Society (https://www.vegsoc.org)
Veganuary (https://veganuary.com)
Viva! (http://www.viva.org.uk)

Index